{ PUT YOUR MOUTH WHERE THE MONEY IS }

swanson•russell

PUT YOUR MOUTH WHERE THE MONEY IS

How to Refocus Your Marketing
Communications for the Greatest
Impact on Sales

Parker Stoner

Publisher | Infusionmedia Publishing

© 2008 Swanson Russell. All rights reserved.

Except for brief quotes used in reviews, no part of this book may be reproduced, stored in a retrieval system, or transmitted in any form, by any means, including mechanical, electronic, photocopying, recording, or otherwise, without prior written permission of the copyright holder.

Infusionmedia Publishing Inc.
140 North 8th Street
205 The Apothecary
Lincoln, NE 68508-1358
www.infusionmediapublishing.com

ISBN 978-0-9796586-7-9

Library of Congress Control Number: 2008938703

10 9 8 7 6 5 4 3 2 1

Contents

Introduction ... vii

{ 1 } CONNECTION

1. What Influences Purchase Decisions? ... 3
2. Hierarchy of Marketing Communications Effectiveness ... 9

LEVEL ONE
3. Actual Experiences with the Brand or Product ... 13

LEVEL TWO
4. Virtual Experiences with the Brand or Product ... 21
5. Recommendations From Trusted Sources ... 25

LEVEL THREE
6. Recommendations From Plausible Sources ... 35
7. Brand/Product News ... 41
8. Active Engagement With/Review of Brand or Product Information ... 43
9. Brand Visibility When and Where Desired by the Audience ... 47

LEVEL FOUR
10. Other Marketing Communications in Acceptable Formats/Environments ... 51

LEVEL FIVE
11. Marketing Communications in Unacceptable Formats/Environments ... 57

{ 2 } PROCESS

12. Marketing Communications for Prospect Audiences ... 63
13. Marketing Communications for Current Customer Audiences ... 71

{ 3 } IDEAS

14. An Introduction to Marketing Communications-Based Product Value Enhancements ... 85
15. Revisiting the Concept of Product Value ... 89
16. The Scope of Marketing Communications ... 93
17. How Marketing Communications Can Add Value to Products ... 95
18. Marketing Communications Ideas to Enhance the Value of Products ... 99
19. Measuring and Evaluating the Success of Marketing Communications-Oriented Product Enhancements ... 115
20. How to Develop Marketing Communications-Oriented Product Enhancements ... 121

INTRODUCTION }

This book is about trust and influence in marketing communications. More importantly, it is about marketers understanding trust and influence in marketing communications so that resources can be allocated where they will have the greatest impact on company revenues. *Put Your Mouth Where the Money Is* describes how marketers can better deploy marketing communications (their "mouth") where they will have the most influence on audience purchases or sales ("money").

This book is also about marketers moving beyond viewing marketing communications as just a tool for delivering messages and conveying brand positioning to an audience. It encourages marketers to consider and aggressively pursue opportunities to use marketing communications as a means of enhancing the actual value of their products, as perceived by customers and prospective customers.

It is essential for marketers to better allocate their resources and better use available marketing communications tools because they are under increasing pressure from top management to demonstrate to the company the bottom-line benefits of their marketing investments.

The following quote from the head of the Association of National Advertisers reflects this pressure:

"While brand building has long been the mantra of marketers, the fundamental meaning of the term has radically changed. No longer are soft measures like 'brand awareness,' 'brand preference' and 'intention to buy' acceptable. Brand building from the C.E.O.'s perspective is about business building—generating higher revenues and profits which will in turn lead to greater shareholder value."

Bob Liodice
Association of National Advertisers[1]

The good news regarding this greater demand for accountability is that it has led to more measurement of marketing communications effectiveness. The bad news is that many marketers have not been pleased with the results of much of that measurement. Often their research shows that their marketing communications are not working as well as they need to work. Key people in the advertising community proclaim that the "old [advertising] model isn't working."

Everyone is aware of the revolutionary changes in media use by consumers and business people during the past 25 years. Gone are the days when most consumers spent their media time with three television networks, a local newspaper, one or two favorite radio stations, and a few general and special-interest magazines. In those days, a business person might have spent significant time with one or two key trade magazines and perhaps a general business magazine. Today there are many more media options—especially in television—competing for audience time and attention. Likewise, the Internet commands an ever-increasing portion of people's time. And it's well known that the less time an individual spends with a given media vehicle, the less likely that individual is to notice the average marketer's advertisement or publicity in that vehicle.

Most marketers have responded to these media consumption changes by either (a) increasing their total marketing communications expenditures so they can have a presence on the Internet and in other new media or (b) shifting some of their marketing dollars from traditional media vehicles to the new media. These strategies certainly make sense, but simply adding or shifting dollars will not solve marketers' challenges.

A 2005 Marketing Receptivity Study by Yankelovich, Inc. concluded that:

"Improvements in marketing practices are far more important to consumers than the greater dissemination of new media. New media are not unwelcome, but by themselves will not engender greater receptivity. The relevant issue is not new versus traditional media; it is old versus new marketing practices."[2]

Most marketing communications in the past were focused on how best to deliver the company's desired message to the target audience as many times as possible for the least cost. Unfortunately, today too many marketers are still stuck in the mindset where the fundamental question is "how do we deliver **our message** to the audience as cost efficiently as possible?"

Today, the audience is less likely to see your message. Even if they do see it, they are unlikely to believe it. Instead, marketers need to frame the question in terms of "how do we invest our marketing communications resources to generate more revenue from the audience or cause behaviors among the audience that will move them closer to making a purchase?" Accomplishing this requires marketers to understand what types of marketing communications have the most believability and influence on audience purchasing and behavior.

There are three main sections of **Put Your Mouth Where the Money Is**:

1. CONNECTION — Why and Where to Reallocate Your Marketing Communications Resources to Better Connect With the Audience

2. PROCESS — Recommended Processes to Implement and Measure Marketing Communications Programs

3. IDEAS — Examples and Ideas for Developing Marketing Communications That Enhance the Value of Your Products

The CONNECTION section of this book presents research regarding the key influences of purchasing activity and the types of marketing communications in which consumers place the most trust. This research is then followed by the *Hierarchy of Marketing Communications Effectiveness*, which shows the relative influence of various categories of marketing communications on purchase activity and product use. We will examine various categories of marketing communications in the *Hierarchy* level by level and provide suggested strategies to use them in the most effective manner.

The PROCESS section builds upon the reallocation strategies to recommend general processes that marketers can implement to communicate and measure the effectiveness of marketing communications programs. Distinct processes are illustrated for communicating with a company's current customers versus prospective customers.

The IDEAS section is more future-oriented in that it encourages marketers to open their minds to the opportunities for marketing communications to add value to their company's products. This section provides a fresh look at the concept of "product value." It highlights six key ways in which marketing communications can enhance the value of products. Then, it goes on to provide examples and ideas of ways in which a variety of online and offline marketing communications tools can be used to enhance product value.

One final point should be made before jumping into this book's specific findings and recommendations. When presented with the data regarding the types of marketing communications that have the greatest and the least influence on consumer purchases, the reaction of many marketers is "the results are obvious." So, if the results are so obvious, why bother with a book describing them and exhorting marketers to reallocate their marketing communications resources? The answer is that while the data may be obvious, a majority of marketers are still allocating the largest percentages of their budgets to the categories of marketing communications with less influence on purchase activity, while placing too little attention on the most influential forms of marketing communications.

Our prescription for marketers is to understand which forms of marketing communications have the greatest influence and reallocate your dollars and other resources to those most influential categories.

Our advice is to **Put Your Mouth Where the Money Is**.

SECTION 1

CONNECTION

Why and Where to Reallocate Your
Marketing Communications Resources
to Better Connect With the Audience

CHAPTER 1

What Influences Purchase Decisions?

What sources of information do people trust? What influences their purchase decisions? Studies consistently show that individuals' past experience with a brand or company have the biggest impact on their decisions to purchase. That is no surprise. The second greatest influences are recommendations and comments from people they know and from other trusted sources. Again, this is not surprising.

Tables 1 through 3 on the following page document consumer trust levels in various types of communications and information sources.

The low ranking for advertising is not surprising. This has been very consistent over the years. The Edelman Trust Barometer, an annual study of the trustworthiness of various resources, confirms the continuing decline in levels of trust of news media.[1]

Historically, there has been an assumption that messages delivered in the media through public relations are more valuable than messages delivered through advertising in the same media because the public relations messages are perceived to be part of the medium's editorial content and thus have greater credibility.

While there is no question about the importance of public relations as a marketing communications tool, the assumption that a message has significantly greater credibility solely because it is delivered through public rela-

TABLE 1
WHAT INCREASES YOUR LEVEL OF TRUST WHEN PURCHASING A PRODUCT OR SERVICE?

Information Source	Percent
Personal experience with the product	81%
Recommendations from others	64%
Reviews by third parties	43%

Source: InsightExpress 2005[2]

TABLE 2
WHAT SOURCES DO CONSUMERS MOST TRUST FOR PRODUCT RECOMMENDATIONS?

Information Source	Percent Who Trust
Friends	65%
Experts	27%
Celebrities	8%

Source: Yankelovich, Inc. 2004[3]

TABLE 3
THINGS YOU HAVE A GREAT DEAL OF CONFIDENCE IN

Information Source	1987	2003
Your own abilities	NA	72%
Doctors	NA	57%
TV News	54%	21%
Newspapers	49%	19%
Web Sites	NA	12%
Information provided by major coporations	29%	12%
News in magazines	37%	9%
Advertising	8%	7%

Source: Yankelovich, Inc. 1987 and 2003[4]

tions should be questioned. As we will examine later, the key is what type of information is being communicated rather than whether it is delivered through advertising or public relations.

According to Forrester/Intelliseek research, only 24 percent of consumers agree with the statement, "companies tell the truth in ads," while 76 percent disagree. The same study highlights what consumers do find valuable about advertising. A total of 73 percent agree with the statement, "ads provide a good way to learn about new products."[5]

The 2004 Yankelovich research reports that 47 percent of consumers agree that "they enjoy advertising." Yet 60 percent of consumers say they try to resist being exposed to marketing and advertising. Further, 69 percent say they are interested in products that allow them to block, skip, or opt out of marketing and advertising.

Table 4 on the next page shows the levels of consumer distrust among various forms of marketing communications. Recommendations from other consumers followed by brand Web sites and e-mail that consumers specifically signed up for have the lowest levels of distrust. The most distrusted forms of marketing communications are e-mail not signed up for, telemarketing, and pop-up advertising.

Most of the available research regarding purchase influences and trust was conducted among consumer audiences. This leads to the question of whether business-to-business audiences are different. In 2007, the Keller Fay Group conducted a study among 700 business executives. It showed that personal experience with a product or service is the number one factor in buying or recommending it with 86 percent saying they recommend a product based on first-hand experience. Further, 50 percent of business executives say they are highly likely to buy a product or service based on recommendations from other business executives.[6]

To summarize this section, consumers most trust and their purchase decisions are most impacted by

1. Themselves and their own experiences with companies/brands.
2. Recommendations/reviews from friends and other known individuals.
3. Recommendations and reviews from credible third parties.

With regard to advertising, consumers say that they tend not to trust it and that they are actively trying to avoid much of it. On the other hand, con-

TABLE 4
U.S. CONSUMER TRUST OR DISTRUST OF TYPES OF MARKETING COMMUNICATIONS

Type of Marketing Communications	Percent Who Distrust*
Recommendations from other consumers	12%
Brand Web sites	27%
E-mail signed up for	34%
Consumer product testimonials online	39%
Newspaper ads	44%
Magazine ads	48%
Radio ads	53%
Television ads	53%
Billboards/outdoor	59%
Brand sponsorships	61%
Search engine advertising	66%
TV-style commercials before movies	72%
Side-by-side product demos in TV ads	73%
Product placement in movies or on TV	73%
Infomercials	79%
Online banner ads	87%
Text-based ads on mobile phones	89%
Door-to-door	92%
Pop-up advertising	94%
Telemarketing	94%
E-mail not signed up for	95%

* Distrust percentage is based on those who say they "distrust somewhat" or "distrust always."

Source: Forrester/Intelliseek 2006[7]

sumers enjoy some advertising and find it valuable as a source to learn about new products. Finally, trust in the traditional news media continues to decline.

Implications for Marketers

There are two key implications of the research regarding trust and purchase influence of marketing communications and information sources:

1. Most marketers are not devoting enough dollars, resources, attention, and creativity to some of the forms of marketing communications that have the greatest influence on consumer purchases.
2. Marketers may be attempting to use some forms of marketing communications—especially advertising—to accomplish goals for which those forms of communications are poorly suited.

CHAPTER 2

Hierarchy of Marketing Communications Effectiveness

Today many marketers allocate their marketing communications resources in ways that are not in the best financial interests of their companies. Often this allocation is done out of habit. Usually the resources are weighted too heavily toward the types of marketing communications, such as advertising and sponsorships, that may be efficient at transmitting messages or brand names, but are not as effective at influencing audience purchases. Further, many marketers use these types of marketing communications in ways for which they are poorly suited. What is needed is a reallocation of marketing communications resources so that a greater portion is devoted to those categories likely to have greater impact on sales.

This unhealthy allocation of marketing communications resources has some similarities to the unhealthy dietary habits of many American consumers. Traditionally, many Americans allowed meat and dairy items to represent much too high a proportion of the foods they consume. Further, many have eaten far too many fats and sweets. To address this situation, the United States Department of Agriculture introduced the USDA Food Pyramid in the 1990s. Although it was modified in 2005, the basic goal of the Food Pyramid was to encourage consumers to change their dietary habits so that they consume a larger portion of healthy grains, vegetables, and fruits, while reducing their intake of dairy, meats, fats, and sweets.[1]

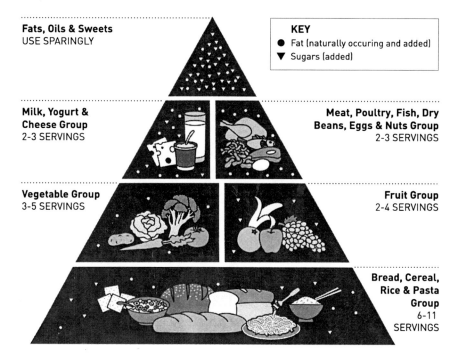

In the same way that many individuals could benefit from a reallocation of their eating priorities, many marketers could benefit from a reallocation of their marketing communications resources so that more are devoted to the most influential categories of marketing communications.

Swanson Russell has developed the *Hierarchy of Marketing Communications Effectiveness* to show key categories of marketing communications and their effectiveness in terms of influence on consumer purchasing. Those forms of communication in the upper levels of the *Hierarchy* have the greatest impact on purchases, while those in the lower levels have less impact. As you can see, five levels are shown.

The purpose of the *Hierarchy of Marketing Communications Effectiveness* is similar to that of the USDA Food Pyramid. It encourages marketers to devote a greater portion of their marketing communications resources to those categories having the greatest impact on purchasing and thus the bottom-line health of a company. The *Hierarchy of Marketing Communications Effectiveness* differs from the Food Pyramid in that the most beneficial activities in the *Hierarchy* are at the top rather than at the bottom, as was the case with the Food Pyramid.

Levels Two and Three show multiple categories of marketing communications. However, this does not mean that these categories are always equal in influence. Especially on the third level, the relative importance of the categories will vary depending upon the product, the audience, and the situation.

The point of the *Hierarchy of Marketing Communications Effectiveness* is not to say that marketers should eliminate all resources applied to the lower levels. In the same way that some meats and dairy products are part of a healthy diet, marketing communications in the lower levels of the *Hierarchy*, when used properly, can be part of a very effective overall marketing communications program. The following chapters will address each of the categories, their rankings, and the implications for marketers.

HIERARCHY OF MARKETING COMMUNICATIONS EFFECTIVENESS

Shown from greatest to least impact on audience purchase or use of a brand.

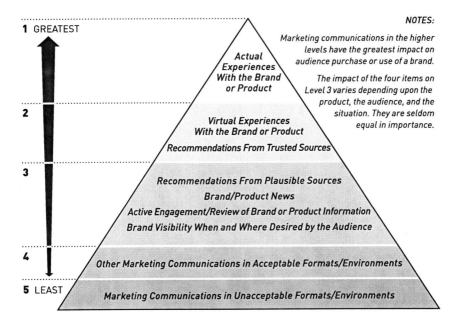

CHAPTER **3**

LEVEL ONE
Actual Experiences With the Brand or Product

We really do not need research data to confirm that actual experiences with the brand or product is the most important factor in determining future use and purchase of a product. It is obvious that if you have used a product and have been happy with it, you will be likely to continue using it and to buy it in the future. If you have been displeased or disappointed with the product, you are much less likely to use it or buy it again.

If this is so obvious, why emphasize the point here? As stated earlier, many companies seem to neglect this fact in the way they allocate their marketing communications resources. They ignore so many things they could be doing in this area and instead devote the majority of their resources to less influential forms of marketing communications.

Another obvious point is that product quality and performance is critical to a good experience. Unfortunately, some marketing communications professionals react to that statement and say "product quality and performance is under the control of Manufacturing or R&D or Quality Control or some other department. There is nothing we can do from a marketing communications perspective to impact the brand or product experience." Nothing could be further from the truth.

Product and brand experiences are made up of far more than the physical product itself. They consist of the total relationship between the consumer and the company, beginning at the time the consumer first makes contact with the company, a dealer, or other representative. That experience continues with the evaluation or consideration process, the purchase process, initial product use, and the ongoing post-purchase interactions the consumer has with the company.

Investing in Initial Touch Points

It is essential to invest marketing resources in those touch points where consumers perceive they are first interacting with your company and products. When consumers take action in response to your advertising, publicity, search engine listings, or recommendations from friends, they are likely to do one or more of the following:

1. Visit your Web site.
2. Visit your store.
3. Call, send an e-mail, or contact your company by mail.
4. Contact or visit a dealer or other sales representative.
5. Attend an event involving your company.
6. Request information or sign up to receive additional communications.

These initial contact experiences need to be better than "good." They need to be outstanding. This is one of the reasons it is so important to invest in a great Web site and to make certain that the Web site is accommodating to first-time visitors. The growth and use of landing pages and microsites tied to specific ads and campaigns reflects the realization by many marketers that it is important to have a smooth transition from the advertising message to the Web site experience rather than simply having first-time prospects go to a Web site home page that is not tied to the ads.

The growth of the World Wide Web has caused some companies to neglect or eliminate the telephone and mail as response options for interested prospects. The arguments for doing so are that handling response inquiries via telephone and mail is more expensive and that "everyone is on the Web." However, not everyone is on the Web. Even among people who have Internet access, many find it more convenient or simply prefer to make initial contact with a company via the telephone or mail. It is important to offer at least a telephone response option, to make sure the people handling incoming calls are well trained, and that processes function smoothly when handling initial prospect contacts.

Swanson Russell has conducted several studies among a variety of companies regarding fulfillment of information requests and inquiries submitted via Web site forms, e-mail, telephone, and mail. Our studies show that 40 to 50 percent of all requests for more information are never successfully fulfilled and that performance is even worse for inquiries submitted via e-mails and Web site request forms. Failure to provide promised information, even after 100 days, makes for a very bad first experience with the company.

Actual delivery of requested information is just the "ante" required to play in the game. Successful inquiry fulfillment and experiences with your company depend upon the quality of the fulfillment efforts. Yes, the quality of the brochures and other materials are important, but prompt fulfillment is even more important. So are (a) including a letter or e-mail message that begins to build a relationship with the prospect and (b) providing a reason to take the next step towards making a purchase.

As a first step, make significant improvements in your inquiry fulfillment and follow-up processes. Then measure your gains in the percentages of leads that convert to trial or purchase. The results should convince you of the importance of implementing such improvements.

The other critical initial touch point for consumers' experiences with your brand or product is interaction with dealers, sales representatives, or other members of the distribution channel.

Obviously, it is essential that your product, in the right size or model when applicable, is available in the store, catalog, or online vendor the prospect visits. So, efforts to expand the number of outlets and breadth of product line carried by those outlets are very valuable.

Moving beyond basic product distribution, the way that your product is displayed in physical or online stores, as well as what retail personnel or sales representatives say about it, also is part of the prospect's experience with the product. All aspects of in-store marketing, including those unique to online stores, not only impact sales volume but also prospects' perceived value and experience with the product. Following are some questions to consider:

1. When a prospective customer asks store or catalog personnel for a recommendation in a product category, do they recommend your company's product?
2. If a prospective customer asks about the quality, performance, durability, or satisfaction with some other aspect of your product, what do the store and catalog personnel say?

3. If a prospective customer asks a question regarding some product feature or other product details, will the store or catalog personnel be able to answer adequately?
4. If a prospective customer displays a moderate level of interest in a competitor product, will the store or catalog personnel encourage that interest or will they suggest that the customer may be even more satisfied with your brand?
5. Do store and catalog personnel say that your product is easy, fun, effective, or whatever other characteristics may be of importance?
6. Do they say that many of their customers have purchased your product and that they have been very pleased with it?

The answers to these and other related questions can have a significant impact on whether your product is purchased and what the perceived value of it is before and after it is purchased. This is especially true when the prospective customer already knows and trusts the store salesperson or when store personnel seems to be knowledgeable regarding the product category.

It is true that as a manufacturer you cannot control what store and catalog personnel say regarding your product during in-store or telephone interactions with prospective customers. However, you can greatly influence that prospective customer experience as it relates to your product. The diagram below shows the process and opportunity.

Regardless of how knowledgeable and helpful a retail or catalog salesperson is, there is always the potential to improve that person's knowledge of, preference for, and attitude regarding your product. Monetary incentives in the form of bonuses, spiffs, or other rewards are one option for improving the situation with salespeople. Building a relationship with and educating store owners, managers, and salespeople is another approach that may be used, alone or in conjunction with monetary incentives.

There are three keys to success in increasing the value of your product through improving customers' in-store or telephone experiences when shopping for it:

1. Make the actual experience of selling and servicing your product the best it can be for store and catalog owners, managers, sales, and service people.
2. Identify and gain access to key store and catalog sales and service people.
3. Effectively communicate with store and catalog people to educate them, create preference, and build an ongoing, mutually beneficial relationship.

We will not attempt to discuss these three keys in detail. With regard to the first key, it is essential for manufacturers to provide easy ordering, prompt delivery, quality service and support, good return policies, and effective marketing support programs. Identifying store owners and managers is usually not difficult unless you sell through distributors that refuse to reveal the stores that carry your products. Identifying individual retail or catalog sales and service people is usually much more difficult. Possible approaches are to

1. Work through the more easily identifiable store owners and managers.
2. Use advertising, publicity, or Web sites to indirectly encourage these individuals to identify themselves.

Developing and distributing basic educational materials regarding your products to store and catalog personnel is an important first step. It is even better to think beyond simple educational materials to consider how you can create real advocates for your products among these people. For example, can you give these individuals a chance to use your products or at least see other people using them successfully? Consider offering them free or discounted samples or opportunities to demo your products. Imagine the credibility and impact that results when a store's salesperson or catalog phone person tells a prospective customer "that's the brand I use." The bottom line is that when distribution channel members are knowledgeable about and advocate your products, the consumer's experience is improved.

The above discussion was focused on retail store and catalog shopping environments. However, the same principles apply to situations in which a salesperson is calling upon prospects. Anything that can be done to better educate salespeople regarding your products, enable them to make better presentations, or do a better job of interacting with prospective customers improves the experience. Thus investments in salesperson training, sales support materials, and sales incentives are strongly encouraged.

Investing in Post-Purchase and Ongoing Customer Relationship-Building Communications

The total experience a consumer has with your product or brand is not limited to the quality and performance of the product. Perceived product value and the consumer's experience are often as much or more a function of the enhancements, extra services, and marketing communications that accompany the product. The opportunities to use various forms of marketing communications to improve the total experience and to increase the value of products are many. Swanson Russell has identified six potential value enhancers that can be delivered through marketing communications:

1. Information
2. Entertainment
3. Convenience
4. Personalization
5. Commemoration
6. Community

These value enhancers can be incorporated into marketing communications tools ranging from product packaging and owners' manuals to Web sites, events, and owners' groups. These tools, when added or dramatically improved, actually enhance the value of the customer's experience with the product. Examples and ideas for using marketing communications will be provided in more detail later in the book.

Let's turn to two valuable, easy-to-implement post-purchase marketing communications activities before leaving this chapter. These are thank-you letters and customer satisfaction surveys.

Thank-You Letters

Many customer-relationship marketing experts cite thank-you letters as the single best relationship-building tool that a company can use. Certainly, it is one of the easiest to implement. Sincere, personalized thank-you letters or notes help customers feel good about your company and their experiences with it. Customers appreciate the effort it takes to send a thank-you **letter** especially since so few companies do this. Consumer surveys show that thank-you e-mail messages, although appreciated, do not have anywhere near the value or impact as mailed letters and notes.

The best thank-you letters are sincere, short, and to the point. They can be used to inform or remind customers of where to go for additional information, to have questions answered, and to resolve any problems. Consider sending occasional thank-you letters or notes throughout the years after customers make a purchase. You never know when customers may be ready to purchase accessories, upgrades, or replacements. Likewise, the customers may know someone else in need of your product. If your customers have been well cared for, they are much more likely to recommend your company.

If you have doubts regarding the return on investment of thank-you communications, test them among a portion of your customers. Then compare the future purchase activity and/or retention rates of those customers against customers who do not receive the thank-you messages.

Customer Satisfaction Surveys

Asking customers about their satisfaction with your company and/or product is another key method of demonstrating that your company cares. Not only can customer satisfaction surveys identify and prevent problems that may damage the customer experience, the act of asking customers about their satisfaction contributes positively to the customer's experience.

There is a particular type of customer satisfaction measure that is gaining popularity with many companies because of its proven, direct link to a company's future growth and success. Management consultant firm Bain & Company found that future company growth correlates very strongly with a simple measure they refer to as the "Net Promoter Score (NPS)."[1]

Your company can determine its NPS by contacting a sample of customers and asking the following question: "How likely would you be to recommend our Company X (or Product X) to a friend or colleague on a scale of 0 to 10 with 10 being extremely likely and 0 being not at all likely?"

Customers answering with a 9 or 10 are classified as "Promoters." Those answering with a 7 or 8 are referred to as "Passives," and those responding with a 0 to 6 are called "Detractors." A company's NPS is calculated by taking the percentage of customers classified as Promoters and subtracting the percentage classified as Detractors. Passives are not figured in the NPS calculation.

NPS = % of Promoters - % of Detractors

For example, if 40 percent of your company's customers answer with a 9 or 10 and 15 percent answer with 0 through 6, your NPS is 25. According to Bain & Company, the average NPS for U.S. companies is less than 10 percent.

The popularity and effectiveness of the NPS approach is due in part to its simplicity and obviousness. Superior products and extraordinary service are the major contributors to a company having large numbers of Promoters and small numbers of Detractors. A high NPS indicates consumers are having positive experiences with the brand and product. Positive experience is the most important factor for determining whether they will purchase your brand and product again.

Also, typically more than 80 percent of a company's positive word-of-mouth communications comes from its Promoters, while most negative word-of-mouth comes from Detractors. These recommendations from trusted sources are the second most important factor in whether someone will purchase.

CHAPTER 4

LEVEL TWO
Virtual Experiences With the Brand or Product

Nothing else is as important as consumers' actual experiences with a brand or product in determining whether they will purchase that same product or other products of the company in the future. There is no complete substitute for the perceptions someone forms as a result of being a customer, whether it is a one-time experience or an ongoing relationship over the course of many years. However, often there are some very effective close approximations for actual experiences. These "virtual" experiences represent the first category on Level Two of our *Hierarchy of Marketing Communications Effectiveness*. There are four primary ways in which marketers can provide individuals with "virtual" or close approximations of actual experiences. These are

1. Free samples
2. Product trials and test drives
3. Viewable product demonstrations
4. Simulated product use

Some of these are better suited to certain products and situations than others. The more that consumers perceive the virtual experience to be representative of the actual customer experience, the greater influence the virtual experience will have on the purchase decision. Obviously, a poor virtual experience can have as significant an impact as a positive one.

Free or reduced-price samples of low-priced, frequently purchased products are a great way to market potentially high-volume products. Sampling is a high, consumer-involvement marketing tool. Consumers often perceive samples as a goodwill gesture on the part of a company. When providing samples, be sure to highlight the benefits and advantages the consumer will experience when using your product. The "power of suggestion" can have an impact on the consumer's experience.

Product trials and test drives in which prospective customers have an opportunity to use the product provide excellent virtual experiences. These tactics are often well suited to big-ticket items and other nonperishable products. While many marketers offer product trials, demonstrations, and test drives, most would benefit from placing more emphasis on employing these tactics. Make it easier for prospects to experience your products and consider providing incentives to do so. Marketers need to make a bigger effort to generate trials and demos than simply having a small line of type at the bottom of an ad that says "Visit your local dealer for a free demo."

Viewable product demonstrations are a good option when it is not feasible for prospects to actually take possession of or consume the product. In some cases, the cost or logistics of bringing the individual and product together in the same location may be prohibitive. In other situations, such as trade shows, when the product and individual are in the same location, the large number of potential prospects or liability issues may make it impractical for each person to actually use the product. Live product demonstrations may be very effective in these circumstances. Other options include televised and online demonstrations. These techniques may not have quite the impact of a live demonstration, but they offer the potential to reach larger, more widely dispersed audiences at their convenience.

Simulated product experiences are possible via Web sites, CD-ROMs, kiosks, and other devices. Kiosks and other devices may be placed in stores, at events, or at other locations. Simulated experiences can have a very high entertainment quality. Sometimes they are offered in the form of a game. Generally, the best simulated experiences make the audience active participants rather than mere spectators. Credibility is not as high for simulated experiences as it is with actual trials or demos, but the entertainment value and convenience will sometimes make them better options.

Virtual experiences with products are high-involvement, high-impact marketing tactics. Regardless of which type of virtual experience is best suited for your product and situation, the overriding point is to use advertising, publicity, and other lower-level communications tools on the *Hierarchy* to drive prospects to these experiences.

Another important point is not to allow the marketing communications effort to begin and end with just the virtual experience. Some virtual experiences lend themselves to pre-event registrations. When that is the case, be sure to communicate with these registrants in advance of the event. Obviously, it is important to resolve any technical or logistical issues well ahead of the event.

Equally important, but often overlooked, is pre-event communications to set expectations, point out key features and benefits to watch for, build a relationship, and make certain that the registered participant does not back out of the event. The form of pre-event marketing communications will vary from regular mail to e-mail and telephone depending on the situation.

There is often much post-experience work to be done in order to obtain a long-term customer. First, be sure to capture the names, addresses, and other pertinent information of people who take part in the virtual experiences. This is valuable for a variety of purposes, including measuring the effectiveness of various advertising and other sources for generating future participants. Second, communicate with the participants after the experience to

1. Obtain their feedback regarding the virtual experience.
2. Answer questions and provide supplemental information.
3. Encourage them to take the next step toward becoming a regular, long-term customer.
4. Track the actions they take.
5. Strengthen the relationship with them to increase the odds that they become a customer.

This process will maximize the value of the virtual experiences and provide you with a measurement of the return on your marketing investment.

CHAPTER **5**

LEVEL TWO
Recommendations From Trusted Sources

The second category on Level Two is *Recommendations From Trusted Sources*. There are two general types of trusted sources:

1. Friends/associates
2. Authorities

The key difference between the two types of trusted sources is whether the consumers personally know the trusted source. Friends and associates are people with whom the consumers have a personal relationship. Trusted authorities are individuals or entities that the consumers know of, but with whom they do not maintain a personal relationship.

Friends/associates can be broadly defined to include family members, acquaintances, work and professional associates, and other people consumers know. Authorities include certain media, organizations, and well-known individuals with whom consumers do not have a relationship. *Consumer Reports* magazine, Oprah, and Ebert & Roper (movies) are well known examples of authorities who are influential among some consumers for some products. Specific writers/editors with print and broadcast media can be trusted sources for many people. Increasingly for some people, a few bloggers are achieving the status of trusted sources regarding particular subjects. Sometimes retail store personnel may be trusted sources when consumers get to know them or simply because they are perceived to be knowledgeable regarding a particular product category.

Recommendations From Friends

The tremendous purchase decision influence of friends, family members, associates, and other people the consumer knows suggests several strategies for marketers. They all revolve around generating very powerful word-of-mouth marketing communications.

1. **Ensure That Customers Have Great Experiences With Your Brand and Products**

This strategy goes back to the top of the *Hierarchy*. If customers are having great experiences with your products, not only does that significantly increase the probability that they will buy from your company again, it also makes them more likely to pass along positive comments to people they know. Realize that there is a big difference between being merely satisfied with a product or brand and being thrilled with it. Customers who are thrilled with a product are much more likely to provide strong endorsements and to be active advocates. That is why Net Promoter Scores are calculated using the customers (Promoters) who rated a 9 or 10 on the likelihood of recommending products to friends, but ignore customers (Passives) who rated a 7 or 8.[1]

2. **Give Current Customers Something to Talk About and Reasons to Talk**

If your company has products that perform very well, as well as very high-quality customer service, you will have a lot of satisfied customers. If their friends ask them about the product and company, those customers will probably respond in a positive way. However, that satisfaction alone will not generate a lot of active, unrequested, word-of-mouth communications on the part of customers.

You need to give customers something worthwhile to talk about and reasons to talk. The word "remarkable" is defined as "being worthy of notice." It applies here. Customers need to be supplied with things that are worth being talked about to their friends. Provide customers with news about new products or services or events that they may pass along to friends. A funny story, a video, or an interesting article regarding your product may provide customers with reasons to spread the word. Try to provide your customers with a frequent supply of news and material that is worth passing along. The more remarkable the material, the more likely it is to be shared with others.

3. Make It Easy for Customers to Spread the Word

Do whatever you can to facilitate customers recommending your product and spreading positive word-of-mouth communications. Make e-mail messages easy to forward. Obvious basic strategies are to include "tell-a-friend buttons" on your e-mail messages and on key pages of your Web site.

Unfortunately, many marketers stop with these few simple-to-implement tools and neglect other methods. Keep in mind that a much larger percentage of consumer recommendations occur face-to-face and over the telephone rather than via e-mail.

According to research from GfK NOP, 80 percent of consumers make product recommendations face-to-face, 68 percent make them over the telephone, and 40 percent use e-mail.[2] Likewise, a 2006 TalkTrak study by the Keller Fay Group showed that 71 percent of word-of-mouth marketing communications occurs face-to-face and 21 percent occurs via telephone. The study reported that just 3 percent occurs via e-mail, 2 percent takes place through instant messaging, and 1 percent occurs in online chatrooms and blogs. Among 13- to 20-year-olds, the e-mail percentage rises to 6 percent and instant messaging increases to 10 percent.[3] So, be sure to supply customers with printed materials, product samples, coupons, and other items they can pass along when face-to-face with other individuals.

4. Consider a Customer Referral Program

There are many variations of customer referral programs ranging from informal and unstructured programs to structured programs with rewards. The most appropriate and effective structure will vary by company and product. The point is to have some type of program—informal or structured—that encourages happy customers to actively recommend your products to their friends. Regardless of whether there are rewards, you should always make a point to personally thank customers when you learn that they made a referral or recommendation.

Generally, low-priced, infrequently purchased products do not lend themselves to structured rewards-based programs because the rewards cannot be of large enough value to matter to customers. Companies selling big ticket items are more likely to be able to justify referral rewards with values of $25, $50, or $100. Rather than just offering a reward to the referring customer, it is usually wise to offer equal rewards to both the current and new customers. Keep in mind that rewards do not have to be limited to cash. They can include premium items, special access/privileges, or anything else of value to the customer and potential customer.

5. Identify and Support Your Strongest Advocates

Every company has a certain percentage of customers who are not merely satisfied with the company, but are genuine fans. These customers will go out of their way to recommend your company's products to friends and other people with whom they come in contact. The enthusiasm and genuineness of these advocates or ambassadors can do a lot for your company's bottom line. Recall the designation of *Promoters* from the earlier discussion of Net Promoter Scores. They are the people who answer "9" or "10" when asked how likely they are to recommend your company to a friend.

It is important to identify these customers and to support their inclination to talk about your company. These advocates are often the people who send in comment cards, sign up to receive newsletters and other information, send you e-mail, or call your company. Customer satisfaction research, such as Net Promoter Score surveys, may be used to identify these advocates. Once you identify them, put their names, addresses, and details obtained from your interactions with them into a marketing database. Regularly thank them for their support, seek their opinions and feedback, supply them with company and product news, offer them logo merchandise, and do whatever else you can to encourage word-of-mouth on their part.

6. Identify and Support Influential Customers

Influential customers are those people that have the widest circle of acquaintances relative to your product category and/or have the most influence among others. Often these are customers who belong to clubs and associations, actively participate in community areas of Web sites, post product reviews on Web sites, attend lots of events, and are looked upon by others as "experts" regarding a particular subject. If you have read Malcom Gladwell's book *The Tipping Point* you may remember his designations of Connectors, Mavens, and Salesmen. *Connectors* are the people with wide social circles. *Mavens* are those people who are very knowledgeable regarding a particular subject. *Salesmen* are charismatic people with the ability to influence others.[4] This framework may be useful when thinking about the most influential customers to identify.

There may be some overlap between influential customers and your strongest advocates. Obviously, someone who fits into both categories is a great asset for your company. As with advocates, it is important to identify these influential customers, enter relevant information about them in a marketing database, and build relationships with them. Do whatever you can to increase their enthusiasm for your company. Also, be sure to resolve any problems or complaints these people have before they express any dissatisfaction among the many people with whom they interact.

7. Identify Vocal Detractors

Research studies show that the economic impact of negative word-of-mouth communications is even greater than that of positive word-of-mouth.

A study by the London School of Economic and Political Science and the Listening Company shows a 7 percent increase in positive word-of-mouth communications unlocks 1 percent additional company growth. On the other hand, a 2 percent reduction in negative word-of-mouth boosts sales by 1 percent. Reducing negative word-of-mouth has more than three times the impact on sales than increases in positive word-of-mouth.[5]

The Customer Dissatisfaction Study conducted by the Verde Group showed that people who heard about someone else's bad shopping experience were even less likely to shop at the offending store in the future than were the people who actually had the negative experience and told friends about it.[6] In addition, a 2005 study by Millward Brown reported that 74 percent of people that heard a personal negative recommendation were influenced to buy a different brand.[7]

The growth of Internet community areas, blogs, and video services such as YouTube have given angry, determined customers the tools to do great damage to your company. So, use your resources to identify these people, resolve the issues that are the root of the negative feelings, and reduce the damage they cause.

Recommendations From Trusted Authorities

Traditional and new media outlets, organizations/associations, and certain well-known individuals can have tremendous influence over the purchasing activities of people. A positive review or rating from one of these sources may elevate a product from "one to consider" to "the top choice," or it may raise a product from "unknown" status to a "serious contender." In a few cases, these trusted authorities may cause devoted followers to purchase a product or brand that they would not have considered otherwise.

Here are some suggested strategies for marketers to capitalize on the influence of trusted authorities:

1. **Get Your Products and Information in the Hands of Trusted Authorities**

Consumers will seek out and listen to the opinions of trusted authorities regarding many products. However, those authorities can only write and talk about your products if they are familiar with them, have received information regarding them, and have an opportunity to use them. Therefore, it is essential that you identify those trusted authorities and then supply them with the samples and supporting information they need to evaluate and communicate about your products. You cannot control what these trusted authorities say about your products, but you can at least make sure they are told about the most important features and advantages.

It is especially important to identify those trusted sources that conduct and publish reviews of your particular product category. Make sure you submit the required samples or information in time to be included in their reviews.

2. **Establish Contact With Trusted Authorities in Traditional Media**

Consumer trust in news media may have decreased in the past 20 years, but it has not completely evaporated. While trust in news media as a whole has declined, many people still have high levels of trust for specific individuals and media vehicles. As a consumer, you may believe that the overall opinions and content of a magazine are influenced by big advertisers, but you still have faith in a particular writer or columnist from that magazine. Simply receiving a mention in a traditional news outlet may no longer have much greater credibility and communications value than an advertisement in the same outlet. But receiving the right kind of review from a specific trusted authority who writes for that outlet can definitely be worth a lot more.

3. **Identify and Contact Important Online Media Outlets**

Many online media and writers are becoming trusted authorities. Their number and influence will only continue to expand in the future. As more of these online outlets incorporate video demonstrations and other multimedia features into their coverage of products, they will gain more influence and greater credibility.

Many of these online media have other advantages when compared to traditional media. Product coverage in a magazine or newspaper, or on television and radio, is usually "gone" once the printed copy is discarded or the program has aired. Product and brand coverage in online media outlets often is archived, where it may be accessed for many years to come.

Online product news, as well as other online media coverage, is often indexed by search engines. Thus, it is visible at critical times by people that use Google, Yahoo!, and other search engines as they seek information regarding particular types of products. It is not unusual to find one or more online media stories regarding a specific product or model that rank higher in keyword search engine rankings than the company's own Web site.

4. Reach Out to Leading Bloggers

Blogs are easy to create and simple to maintain or abandon. Anyone can create a blog in a matter of minutes. That is why there are millions of them and why many more are created each day. As a category, blogs do not have a high degree of credibility. However, many individuals come to know and develop trust in a few select blogs. So some blogs have significant readership and influence with individuals.

The people that are active readers of and/or contributors to blogs regarding a particular subject tend to be among the more influential people on that subject. Blogs may represent a significant source of the information that they use to maintain their status as having insider information. They pass that information along to other individuals through online and offline word-of-mouth communications. So it is valuable to reach out to key bloggers, not only because of the size of their immediate audience but also because active blog participants tend to be influential.

Blogs began as text-based endeavors, possibly with some supporting photos. Today many have expanded into more multimedia vehicles using video and other tools. Also, some individuals have introduced video blogs in which most or all of the content is in video rather than written form. Marketers need to understand that their products will often be reviewed in video form and that the video may not always be of the highest quality. Additionally, marketers should be prepared to meet the needs of this new breed of trusted authorities by making product information available to them in a video format.

One last point should be made regarding blogs. They are having an increasing impact on search engine results. Often blog entries will rank among the highest results on keyword searches. Further, the greater the number of blogs and other Web sites that link to your company's Web site, the more it helps raise your company's Web site search engine rankings.

5. Pay Attention to Active Online Social Network Participants

Lately, marketers, media, and online entrepreneurs have been on a mission to establish online community forums. Millions of Web sites have some form of online bulletin board, chat room, or forum. In most cases, the participants consist of (a) a small but vocal group that tends to dominate the conversation, (b) the "courageous" newbies who occasionally ask questions and seek advice, and (c) the larger group of lurkers who view postings of the first two groups but rarely contribute.

The important consideration for marketers is that the small but vocal group that dominates the conversation is often very opinionated and influential. Over time, some of them become trusted authorities within the community. It makes sense for marketers to locate the most widely used online community sites relative to their product categories, identify the small group that dominates the conversation, and reach out to those people in an effort to improve their experiences with and opinions of your products. This same strategy also applies to individuals who are active participants and posters to influential blogs originated by other people.

6. Have an Effective Public Relations Program in Place and the Necessary Resources to Execute It

The five strategies described above involve a lot of work and require the dedication of many resources to be effective. This is not quick, easy work. The key point of this book is that the marketing communications activities on the highest levels of this *Hierarchy of Marketing Communications Effectiveness* are the most critical ones in influencing purchases of your products. Therefore, if dollars and other resources are limited—as they always are—it is best to take some resources devoted to activities at lower levels of the *Hierarchy* and redeploy them to activities on the higher levels of the *Hierarchy*. Put another way: Don't skimp on the types of public relations activities described in the first five strategies above.

The most effective public relations programs usually employ a combination of internal resources and outside professional assistance. A public relations program that does little more than distribute a few new product news releases puts your company at a major competitive disadvantage. Outside professional public relations assistance can increase your reach and effectiveness to the ever-expanding assortment of trusted authorities. If they have deep experience in your industry, they probably know and have relationships with trusted authorities your company does not know. At the very least, outside professionals may have more time and better skills at locating and establishing contact with these people.

One other point should be made regarding the ever-expanding networks of trusted authorities and how to best maintain relationships with them. Back when the media and trusted authorities for a particular industry were small in number, it was relatively easy for companies or their outside public relations agents to maintain very personal one-to-one relationships with them. Companies and/or their outside support could have fairly frequent telephone contact and occasional face-to-face meetings with the key authorities.

Now it is just not realistic to have that same frequency and type of personal contact with the expanded network of trusted authorities that include online media, bloggers, social network influentials, and others. What may be called for is employing database marketing communications structures and approaches in combination with public relations strategies to build and maintain personalized dialogues with the vast network of trusted authorities.

7. Publicize and Advertise Positive Reviews by Well-Known Trusted Authorities

The research findings that form the foundation for this book stressed that most consumers do not find the claims made in advertising to have a lot of credibility. As will be discussed later, the effectiveness and wisdom of using advertising to communicate your company's claims about its products is questionable. On the other hand, there is value in informing consumers about positive reviews of products on the part of well-known trusted authorities.

This can be a very effective use of advertising and news releases because these messages do not require that consumers trust the claims of the marketer regarding the product. Instead, consumers only need believe that a trusted authority commented on a product. Especially on the Internet, it is often possible and easy for consumers to verify that the trusted authority actually made the positive comments.

It is valuable for marketers to use online and offline advertisements and news releases to point or link consumers to locations where they may find the actual independent positive statements of the trusted authorities. Even if this type of news release is never published in a major media outlet, it still has great potential value if it is placed on the company's own Web site. There it may be viewed by many consumers and indexed by search engines.

CHAPTER 6

LEVEL THREE
Recommendations From Plausible Sources

Level Three is the middle zone of the *Hierarchy*. The categories of marketing communications on this level are not as influential in consumer purchasing as are the categories in the top two levels. However, Level Three communications are more influential than those at the lower levels. What is interesting is that many of the categories on Level Three represent the same types of communications, such as media advertising, publicity, and company marketing materials, that are also found on Level Four. However, when these types of marketing communications are infused with certain types of content or are offered in certain environments, they take on greater importance and credibility for the audience. That is why they are shown on Level Three rather than Level Four.

It bears repeating, as we begin to explore Level Three, that the relative importance and influence of the categories of marketing communications at this level will vary from one product category to another. For some companies, *Recommendations From Plausible Sources* may have more influence among prospective customers, while *Brand Visibility Where and When Desired by the Audience* will be more important for others.

The first Level Three category is *Recommendations From Plausible Sources*. A plausible source is someone who seems to have relevant, unbiased knowledge of a product or company even though the person is not known personally by the consumer nor is the person an established trusted authority. Examples of plausible sources are

1. Individuals who express an opinion or relate their experience with a product in an online social networking environment.
2. People who post reviews in online stores, such as Amazon.com and Cabelas.com, or Web sites, such as Trip Advisor, that feature consumer reviews.
3. Individuals shown and/or quoted in company advertisements, on Web sites, and in other materials.

These sources are plausible if they are perceived to be (a) real people using/experiencing the product under conditions similar to what the consumer anticipates she would encounter and (b) providing genuine comments that are not based on any financial compensation, other ties to the company, or any ulterior motives.

The following are some suggested marketing strategies for capitalizing on the potential of recommendations from plausible sources.

1. Take Advantage of the Research Value of Online Comments

Visit some of the key Internet sites where people are commenting on your company, your products, and your competitors.

1. What are they saying?
2. Are there negative comments that point out weaknesses in your products or service that need to be fixed?
3. Are there certain positive comments that are made frequently? Perhaps some of these themes can be incorporated into your advertising and other marketing communications.
4. Look for comments that indicate unmet needs. Can your company do something to meet them?
5. Online comments may not have the statistical validity of a $100,000 research study that represents the entire marketplace. However, they can provide real insight into audience perceptions of your product. And it does not take $100,000 to obtain them.

2. Identify and Build Relationships With Prominent Online "Talkers"

Who are the most influential "talkers" when it comes to your product category? Find the Web sites and other online destinations that have the largest numbers of active participants commenting about your product category and related subjects. Identify people in online social communities that fit into these categories (some people may be in more than one category):

1. Strong advocates of your company and products.
2. Individuals that have made some positive comments regarding your company or products.
3. The most respected and influential individuals.
4. The most frequent "talkers," regardless of whether they are respected.
5. People actively badmouthing your company or products.
6. Individuals describing a negative experience with your company.

Each of these categories of talkers needs to be approached using a unique strategy. Thank those people who have made positive comments and make sure they are aware of your products, services, and information resources such as Web sites and newsletters. Ask for feedback from the most active "talkers." They will likely appreciate having an audience for their views. Apologize and make amends for legitimate negative experiences when possible.

Generally, it is best to approach "talkers" privately through an individual message rather than posting a message viewable to the entire forum. You do not want to offend those people who are your supporters or to damage their credibility. At the opposite end, you need to avoid supplying active detractors with more ammunition. You do not want to be perceived as attempting to "buy" their loyalty or silence.

3. Give Special Attention to Reviews Posted in Online Stores

Imagine this scenario. A prospective customer has seen your advertising, visited your Web site, and is now headed to his favorite online retailer with intention to buy your product. He sees that the price is acceptable. Before adding your product to his "shopping cart," he stops to read some of the reviews posted by other customers. If the reviews are favorable, that prospect adds the product to his shopping cart, completes the purchase, and becomes your customer. However, if that prospect encounters several negative or disappointing reviews about the product or service support, he may stop dead in his tracks. He may delay his purchase in order to do further evaluation or he may switch to a more positively rated competitor's product.

A somewhat different scenario could involve a prospective customer who wants to buy a particular type of product but is undecided regarding the brand. So, this prospect visits her favorite online store to evaluate the options. Most likely price will be a factor. Available styles, colors, and models may play a role, too. Online reviews from plausible sources at the point of purchase have tremendous power to influence her purchase in these situations.

For years marketers have understood the power of point-of-purchase advertising in traditional retail stores because of the exposure immediately before purchase. Imagine if instead of encountering a sign or display in a store, the customer found next to the shelf with your product five other customers holding signs saying, "I've used this product; ask me about my experience." Their comments would have much greater influence on the purchase decision than any typical point-of-purchase materials.

That is why online reviews from plausible sources may be an even more influential form of point-of-purchase communications for Internet shoppers. So it is important to be aware of and address these types of reviews in your company's marketing communications programs.

The types of comments found in online store reviews tend to be different than those found in Internet social communities. Online store product reviews tend to be more focused and tend to have less ranting and raving. Still, you find many of the same categories of reviewers as were listed in the section for online social communities. The same advice given in that section holds true here as well.

4. Consider Publishing or Linking to Positive Customer Comments From Other Web Sites

Can you publish or link to positive customer comments regarding your products on other Web sites? In many cases the owners of the other sites will allow this. They may even appreciate the added publicity and traffic driven to their site. In other cases, the answer will be "no." The site owners may resent attempts to use their sites for your commercial gain. Sometimes membership sign-in or access requirements to an online social site may prevent direct links to the content by nonmembers.

5. Participate in Online Communities

Encourage your employees to participate in key online communities, but to do so in an acceptable way. Their participation should not be viewed as an opportunity to aggressively promote your company or its products. Attempts to do so will almost certainly backfire and create animosity. The best approach is to actively participate in the community in a positive way unrelated to your brand. Offer helpful advice, ask questions, and so on. Listen and learn.

How does this seemingly neutral participation lend itself to productive marketing communications for your company? Employee participants should be upfront about who they are and their affiliation with your company. If allowed, include this information in their online signature and profile. Each time that employee posts a message, it creates awareness of your company and adds credibility.

Other community regulars and visitors who see that your employee is a regular participant will be more likely to post comments or questions regarding your company to which your employee may respond in a positive, but honest, manner. Any comment or question regarding your company or a need that your products can meet becomes an opportunity for your employee to respond. Setting the record straight, fixing a problem, or otherwise contributing to the online community helps negate the impact of negative comments from detractors and provides a positive experience with your company for current and prospective customers.

6. Build Your Own Online Community

You can strengthen customers' relationships with and loyalty to your company if you give them a forum to communicate with each other. Establishing an online community is a way of enhancing the total value of your products for customers. Also, it can be a valuable tool for positively influencing prospective customers.

Assume that a prospect is interested in your company's product. He visits your Web site to learn more about specifications, available sizes or models, and other characteristics. While at the Web site, he discovers he can read comments from other customers and perhaps ask some questions of actual product users. If he sees mostly positive comments and genuine enthusiasm, he is much more likely to proceed to buy your company's products.

Establishing and maintaining a quality online community is not an inexpensive undertaking nor is it a simple process. However, it can be a very worthwhile investment—especially if you have a large, enthusiastic base of customers with reasons to talk.

7. Use Real Customer Comments in Advertising, on Web Sites, and in Other Marketing Materials

Testimonial advertising has a long history of demonstrated effectiveness. Today there are many more ways of publicizing positive customer comments and experiences. In addition to traditional uses in advertisements, brochures, and catalogs, consider sharing positive comments on your Web site, in podcasts, in e-mail newsletters, and in other new media.

Most of the ideas in this section of *Recommendations From Plausible Sources* have focused on online media. Certainly, this will be the source of many customer comments. However, do not forget other sources of positive and negative comments, including letters to your company, comment cards, phone calls, and letters to the editor published in magazines. Establish a system for collecting, responding to, evaluating, and using both online and offline customer comments.

CHAPTER 7

LEVEL THREE
Brand/Product News

Legitimate news regarding a brand or product is valuable to audiences. They pay attention to this type of information and find it credible. An advertisement, news release, Web site, direct mail piece, e-mail message, or brochure that claims a product is "the best in its category," "the one you need," "dollar-for-dollar the best value," or some other carefully crafted line has very little credibility with most people. It will not be believed and will likely be ignored. On the other hand, an advertisement, news release, or other communication that announces a new product, service, significant enhancement, or opportunity to experience the product has much greater credibility and generates more interest among an audience.

The fact that something new has been introduced or that a product is now available at a specific location generally is believable. A claim that it is better than others or will make the consumer's life wonderful is typically met with skepticism or ignored.

Most marketers do make a point of using advertising, publicity, and other forms of marketing communications to highlight new products and other major news. Where they often fail is in converting the audience attention to the news into action that moves interested prospects closer to purchase. Much of the time the communications are so focused on delivering the news and other associated messages that they neglect to provide specific guidance regarding what action the audience should take next and a compelling reason to do so. Advertisements that just list a phone number or Web site in small type at the bottom or end of the message are prime examples of this.

Value to the company does not come from delivering the news to an audience. Marketing value comes from the actions some members of the audience take that move them, or other people they influence, closer to making a purchase.

Sale prices, rebates, discounts, and other special offers also constitute "news." They capture audience attention but sometimes lack credibility. Audiences have come to expect a "catch" or qualifier that downgrades the value of the offer. Communications that give offer specifics, including exact prices, and that lack asterisks leading to qualifiers help overcome the skepticism.

Likewise, online and in-person events represent "news." Advertising and publicity that highlight events in which there will be an opportunity to experience the brand, interact with current customers, or learn more about a subject of interest related to the product category tend to generate greater interest and have more credibility.

The key point here is that there is a huge difference in effectiveness between advertising, publicity, and other marketing communications in the "news" category compared to the same types of marketing communications that simply deliver a claim, a slogan, or other message from the company. That is why *Brand/Product News* is on Level Three of *The Hierarchy of Communications Effectiveness*.

Most ads, publicity, and so on that primarily deliver a claim, slogan, or other message are one level down on the *Hierarchy* and belong in the category *Other Marketing Communications in Acceptable Formats/Environments*. They will be discussed further in a later chapter.

Advertising practitioners from John Caples to David Ogilvy have trumpeted the effectiveness of advertisements that feature legitimate news. Media are much more likely to publish company news releases that highlight real news. News generates interest. It has credibility. It gets passed along from person to person, making it the basis of some of the best word-of-mouth or viral marketing. Invest your money in marketing communications that deliver news of significance to your audience.

CHAPTER 8

LEVEL THREE
Active Engagement With/Review of Brand or Product Information

There is a significant difference in value to a company between an individual just being exposed to your ads, news releases, or other marketing communications materials versus actively seeking and interacting with your brand information. Individuals that have elected to actively engage with your brand in one way or another are expressing a greater level of interest and will likely find the message to be more credible than if they were just exposed to it through other media. The combination of time commitment by the person, heightened interest, and greater perceived message credibility adds up to greater value for marketing communications that fits within this category.

It is important to make a distinction here between (1) *Actual Experiences With the Brand or Product*, (2) *Virtual Experiences With the Brand or Product*, and (3) *Active Engagement With/Review of Brand or Product Information*. The first two categories involve actual or virtual use of the product itself and thus are higher on the *Hierarchy of Marketing Communications Effectiveness*. The third category is limited to engagement with brand or product **information** rather than the product itself. *Active Engagement With/Review of Brand or Product Information* is much more influential in the purchase process than simple message exposure, but not as influential as actual or virtual use of the product.

Here are some examples of *Active Engagement With/Review of Brand or Product Information*:

1. Visiting a Web site.
2. Requesting additional information or materials via mail, telephone, fax, e-mail, online, or in some other way.
3. Clipping or downloading a coupon.
4. Contacting or visiting a dealer or other distribution channel member.
5. Picking up and reviewing company literature or materials while in a store, at an event, or somewhere else.
6. Engaging with a kiosk, point-of-purchase materials, or other form of display.
7. Attending an event at which current customers of the brand, information regarding the brand, or the brand itself will be present.
8. Interacting with brand information or representatives of the brand at a booth or seminar at a trade show, consumer show, or similar event.
9. Signing up for a company's newsletter, e-mails, alerts, or some other ongoing information services.
10. Actively engaging with involvement devices such as quizzes, games, scented strips, removable stickers, or other items contained in a printed or digital advertisement, direct mail piece, brochure, or other company materials.

Each of the above examples—as well as many other items which could be listed—is valuable to the company because the audience has undertaken some behavior to actively seek information or engage with the brand. This is a significant step up from merely seeing, listening to, reading, or otherwise being exposed to an advertisement, news release, or other marketing communication that has reached the audience. Obviously, an advertisement that is paid attention to or read provides more value to the company than one that is only noticed. However, it will not have the greater impact and credibility among the audience—or value to the marketer—that is achieved when the person actively seeks or engages with the brand information.

The advice here is not to employ tactics that stop at just delivering a message—especially in an environment where the audience is likely more interested in the program or editorial content than your message. Move beyond a goal of "exposing the audience to your message" and strive for "engaging the audience with your brand" through some action on their part.

CHAPTER 9

LEVEL THREE
Brand Visibility When and Where Desired by the Audience

We have entered an era in which people want to and expect to obtain information whenever and wherever they want it. The growth of the Internet is the biggest reason for this change in expectations. Need to find something? Just "Google" it.

Often annoyed by the volume of marketing messages pushed out to them, consumers sometimes will go to great lengths to avoid unwanted messages. But when they want information or want to locate a product, they want to do so right away. Thus, there is greater perceived value and credibility for marketing information that is easily accessible when and where the audience wants it.

Years ago, advertising in the "Yellow Pages" directory was the best example of having a company's brand visible—when and where the audience wanted it. When individuals wanted pizza, golf clubs, garden supplies, or any of thousands of other products, they opened the "Yellow Pages" to find the available choices. Business listings and advertisements in telephone directories are still an important place for brand visibility when and where audiences want it. But clearly, the Internet has become dominant.

Now, search engine rankings are critical for almost every marketer. When individuals enter your company or brand name in Google, Yahoo!, MSN, or one of the other search engines, your listing had better appear at or near the top of the first page of results. Likewise, when individuals enter your product category or other related search terms, the higher your company ranks among the listings, the better for your business. Keep in mind that your company's presence in blogs, online news, and other content also will impact search engine rankings.

This book is not the place to discuss the hundreds of techniques for improving search engine rankings or debating organic versus paid search. There is a wealth of other information regarding these subjects. For now, we will simply say that search engine marketing should be a very important part of most companies' marketing communications programs.

Here are a few other examples of providing brand visibility when and where the audience desires:

1. Listings or ads in special directory, gift guide, or product category review issues of consumer or trade magazines. These types of special issues are more likely to be saved. Special articles may be torn out or scanned for future reference.
2. Listings or ads in printed or online catalogs that include your product category.
3. Booths or displays at consumer shows, trade shows, and other events that individuals attend, in part, to learn about products.
4. Point-of-purchase materials and displays that provide product information at the time and location when consumers are ready to purchase.

Other examples could be listed that are somewhat unique to specific product categories. Keep in mind that it is critical to stay on top of technology and other developments that impact when, where, and the format in which consumers expect to access information. For example, as the use of wireless devices grows, consumers will expect to access more information through them. Displays designed for viewing on larger computer screens may not be suitable for viewing on smaller wireless devices.

The key point regarding search engine listings, telephone directories, and the other brand visibility examples is that marketing communications in these areas are likely to have greater impact on consumer purchasing than ads and other messages that are pushed out to the audience through the usual print, broadcast, and digital channels. It is a difference of information being available when and where the audience wants it rather than when and where the marketer or media dictate it. Both have their places in the marketing communications mix, but there is greater acceptance when audiences are seeking them.

CHAPTER **10**

LEVEL FOUR
Other Marketing Communications in Acceptable Formats/Environments

This rather vaguely titled category probably contains a larger portion of most companies' marketing communications expenditures than any other category in the *Hierarchy of Marketing Communications Effectiveness*. It includes the majority of media advertising, whether print, broadcast, outdoor billboards, direct mail, or digital advertising on the Internet. Most product placements and sponsorships, plus some publicity, also fall into this category.

The key phrase that distinguishes marketing communications in this category is "acceptable formats/environments." Most consumers accept the trade-off of receiving newspaper, magazine, radio, and television news and entertainment for free or at a low price in return for advertisements being placed in these media. Most people do not object to sponsor logos and brief messages appearing at sports, entertainment, or other events. Likewise, the majority of (a) product placements in television and movies, (b) direct mail pieces, and (c) marketer-originated stories appearing in media do not raise objections from people.

This acceptance by most consumers is what separates marketing communications in this category from those in the Level Five category, *Marketing Communications in Unacceptable Formats/Environments*, to be discussed later. Certainly, people may object to the number of marketing communications messages in these acceptable formats and environments or to the content of a few messages. And many people are actively seeking ways to more easily avoid exposure to so many messages by using digital video recorders (DVRs) and other devices. Still, marketers generally will not anger consumers or cause negative feelings toward their brands just because they insert marketing messages into these environments.

So, why are these forms of marketing communications in a Level Four category that is near the bottom of the *Hierarchy*? What differentiates them from marketing communications at the higher levels? It is their lack of credibility and lower effectiveness at impacting audience purchase or use of a brand. Refer to the research studies at the beginning of this book that show low confidence in advertising, the news media, and major corporations for a reminder as to why this is so.

Let's be clear about three key points:

1. "Lower" credibility and impact on purchasing does not mean "no" credibility or influence on purchasing.

The five levels in the *Hierarchy* do not mean that marketing communications in the lower levels have no credibility or ability to impact purchases. Rather, they tend to have less credibility and impact on purchasing compared to marketing communications in the higher levels. Often the differences in impact are very big.

2. Not all media advertising, sponsorships, and publicity are in Level Four of the *Hierarchy*.

Media advertising that merely seeks to deliver a brand message or convey an image falls into this *Other Marketing Communications in Acceptable Formats/Environments* category. Advertising that announces new products and services, informs interested individuals of opportunities to experience the brand, or helps them to connect with credible sources of information are on a higher level of the *Hierarchy*. An advertisement that announces a new product or informs people about a time, location, and means of learning more about a product has greater credibility.

Claims that a product is "the standard in quality," "first in service," or "the right choice" are not credible. Similarly, marketing communications messages such as "get on board," "enjoy the good life," or "discover the new you" may be appealing, but, by themselves, have little credibility or power to move people closer to making a purchase. Unfortunately, a majority of advertising seems more concerned with creating awareness or recall of these types of messages.

Sponsorship arrangements that do nothing more than give exposure to a brand name, logo, or slogan, or that tell people "Brand X is the official bottled water of the NBA" have little impact on purchasing. While they have some value and are not objectionable, they do not help facilitate marketing communications at the higher levels of the *Hierarchy*. On the other hand, a sponsorship arrangement that gives audiences an opportunity to sample or test drive a product, ask questions, obtain more information, or interact with current customers of the brand has much greater value. These sponsorships move up into Level Two and Level Three of the *Hierarchy* rather than Level Four.

The bulk of publicity published in major news media rises above this fourth level of the *Hierarchy* into the third level. That is because a majority of what gets published contains some legitimate news regarding the product and therefore is of value to some of the audience. This type of publicity is especially valuable if it contains information that facilitates interested individuals obtaining more information or engaging with the product.

Other publicity efforts will even reach Level Two of the *Hierarchy* because they will result in positive reviews or recommendations from magazine writers or other individuals that are trusted sources for much of the audience. This type of publicity is worth its weight in gold. At the opposite end of the spectrum, negative reviews from trusted sources can be very damaging.

The type of publicity that falls down to Level Four of the *Hierarchy* is publicity that does not provide any significant news about the company or product and is not attributed to trusted sources. Publicity that only gets a company's name or product mentioned, or conveys something of little use to the audience, falls down to this fourth level of the *Hierarchy*. While the audience will not react negatively to this type of exposure, it offers no special credibility or value.

The belief that this type of exposure is so many more times valuable than advertising just "because it is *free* PR" does not have merit—especially given the dramatic declines in consumer trust of media. That quarter-page photo of your company president shaking hands with someone at a trade show three months ago does not automatically provide greater credibility or marketing value than a quarter-page advertisement in the same magazine that announces a new product. The fact that the photo is "PR" does not mean it is more valuable than advertising. The same is true for other publicity that does not provide any news of value to the audience.

3. *Entertainment appeal* and *message memorability* are not the same as *marketing value.*

Many ads, especially those on television and radio, are very entertaining. People enjoy hearing and seeing them. Likewise, many people enjoy the beautiful graphics or artistry in some print ads, direct mail pieces, and other marketing materials. Other advertising becomes memorable, especially when the audience is exposed to it over time.

It is good for advertisements to be entertaining, attractive, or memorable. But they still will not have the same credibility or ability to directly impact a person's purchasing as will the person's actual experience with the product or recommendations from trusted sources. Advertising that merely entertains or is visually appealing produces limited marketing value for the company. The marketing value comes when that entertainment or visual appeal is used to help capture attention in order to convey news or help the audience obtain information, recommendations, and experiences that are credible.

Strategies for Utilizing Other Marketing Communications in Acceptable Environments

The point of this chapter is not that marketers should stop using advertising, sponsorships, and other marketing communications in this category. The advice is to use these types of marketing communications in the ways that make them effective tools for your company rather than wasteful ones. Also, make sure that your marketing communications funding and resource allocation is not bottom heavy, with the majority falling into this lower level. Be sure that you are devoting sufficient resources to marketing communications in the upper levels of the *Hierarchy.*

Here are some specific recommendations for improving the value of marketing communications so that they rise into the higher levels of the *Hieararchy*:

1. Use advertising and publicity when you have new products, services, and significant enhancements to announce.
2. Establish and identify opportunities for prospective customers to experience your products or interact with current enthusiastic customers. Use advertising and publicity to inform audiences about these opportunities.

3. Devote more attention, real estate, or time in advertisements to providing audiences with reasons to respond or take actions that move them toward product trial.
4. Look for sponsorship packages that give your company opportunities to connect the audience with your product, distribution channel representatives, and customer advocates.
5. Avoid wasteful spending on advertising, publicity, sponsorships, and other marketing communications that only expose your brand name, logo, tagline, or unsubstantiated claims.
6. Devote resources to public relations activities that are likely to yield positive reviews and recommendations from influential, trusted writers, bloggers, and other media members.

CHAPTER **11**

LEVEL FIVE
Marketing Communications in Unacceptable Formats/Environments

We have now reached the bottom of the *Hierarchy of Marketing Communications Effectiveness*. This category includes types of marketing communications that significant numbers of consumers find objectionable. The fact that a marketing communications tool falls into this category does not mean that it cannot ever be effective or that it never has any impact on purchasing. However, use of these marketing communications tools runs the risk of angering or alienating current and prospective customers. Some of the marketing communications that fall into this category include

1. Outbound telemarketing
2. Spam e-mail
3. Pop-up Internet ads
4. Door-to-door sales
5. Unrequested communications on mobile phones and faxes
6. Advertisements in objectionable locations

A few comments are in order for some of these items. When talking about telemarketing, it is important to distinguish between outbound versus inbound telemarketing, and then between desirable and undesirable forms of outbound telemarketing. Consumers welcome the ability to call a company for more information or to have questions answered when they want to do so. This is inbound telemarketing. On the other hand, consumers find much unsolicited outbound telemarketing initiated by or on behalf of companies to be objectionable. However, some outbound calls by companies are positive. For example, follow-up calls by companies to confirm receipt of materials requested by consumers or to answer their questions are generally positive.

There is a huge difference in consumer reactions to desired e-mail and undesired e-mail (spam). Recall from the research at the beginning of this book that *e-mail not signed up for* ranked dead last in terms of trust. It was even worse than telemarketing. On the other hand, *e-mail signed up for* ranked third in trust: only behind recommendations from other consumers and brand Web sites. Other research confirms that e-mail signed up for is welcomed, while unsolicited e-mail is hated. And, as the volume of e-mail grows, consumer annoyance with unsolicited e-mail increases. Send spam to consumers and they will almost certainly avoid your company. They may even take active steps to hurt your company.

The big challenge for marketers with e-mail is that there is a fine, often hard-to-determine line between what consumers consider to be desirable versus spam e-mail. According to 2008 research from Q Interactive

1. 56 percent of consumers consider marketing messages from known senders to be spam if the message is "just not interesting to me."
2. 50 percent of consumers classify "too frequent messages from companies I know" to be spam.
3. 31 percent agree that "e-mails that were once useful, but aren't relevant anymore" are spam.[1]

This suggests that companies that send e-mails need to be aggressive in confirming that subscribers want to continue receiving e-mails and to make it easy to opt out.

There is danger, as well, for marketers who use e-mail lists from list suppliers even when the people on the list supposedly opted in to receive e-mail from other companies. The consumer who, a year ago, happened to check a box as part of a sign-up process for some other organization's materials will not make the connection between that "opt-in" and the e-mail message your company is now sending. To that consumer, your company's e-mail message is most likely perceived as unsolicited and unwelcome.

Some readers may be surprised to see that direct mail is not on the list of *Communications in Unacceptable Formats/Environments*. Many people refer to direct mail as "junk mail." Some people immediately toss out unwanted direct mail pieces with little more than a brief glance. However, with the exception of a small percentage of the population with major criticisms over paper waste in direct mail, few people object to receiving direct mail, even when unsolicited. In fact, research shows that direct mail is experiencing a resurgent acceptance and popularity among many consumers. Surprisingly, the growth of e-mail is a key factor in the improved consumer perceptions of direct mail.

Four times since 1999, International Communications Research and Pitney Bowes conducted consumer surveys regarding direct mail and e-mail preferences. The latest survey from 2007 showed that

1. 73 percent of consumers prefer mail for receiving product announcements and offers from companies with whom they currently do business. Only 18 percent prefer e-mail.
2. 70 percent prefer mail for receiving unsolicited information from companies with whom they do not currently do business.[2]

Consumers say direct mail is less intrusive, more convenient, less high pressured, more descriptive, and more persuasive than e-mail. Other research shows that consumers, including the young ones, recognize the greater costs and efforts incurred by companies communicating with them by direct mail compared to e-mail.

SECTION 2

PROCESS

Recommended Processes to
Implement and Measure Marketing
Communications Programs

CHAPTER **12**

Marketing Communications for Prospect Audiences

The primary point of this book is that marketers should move more of their marketing communications resources away from the categories on the lower levels of the *Hierarchy* and allocate more resources to the categories in the higher levels. Marketing communications activities in the higher-level categories are likely to have a greater influence on audience purchases and use of your products.

At this point, you should understand the essence of this book and the reasons for our recommendations, as well as have some basic strategies for better utilizing a variety of communications tools. Going forward, it is helpful to have an overall marketing communications process to follow in order to incorporate the recommendations presented in the book's first section.

While it is impossible to develop a specific process that meets the unique needs of all companies, we can at least provide a general process that may give you a good foundation to build upon. What follows in the next two chapters are two charts—one for prospects and one for customers—that depict a process along with strategies and key metrics at each step.

The Prospect Marketing Communications Chart on page 66 displays a three-step process starting with initial communications contact and ending, hopefully, with product purchase. The process may be thought of as a funnel that is wide at the top and that narrows as we move downward. This is because

Step 1 of the process includes all of a company's prospects, while only a portion of those prospects complete the downward journey to the desired end.

Step 1. Reach Out to Prospects and Generate Action

At the start of the process, the company's general marketing communications strategy is to reach out to potential prospects and provide reasons why those prospects may be interested in the product or company. However, this awareness creation or message delivery alone is not enough to provide value to the company or to the prospects. It is essential as part of the strategy to persuade interested prospects to learn more, try the product, experience the brand, or take some other step toward purchase. Without this action, prospects remain at the top of the chart.

The activities in this first step of the process can be grouped into four categories:

Active Direct Tactics

Active direct tactics that are used by a marketer to communicate directly with prospects include print, broadcast, digital, direct mail, and other forms of advertising along with publicity, sponsorships, events, and other communications tactics.

Active Indirect Tactics

Active indirect tactics are those activities designed to persuade distribution channel members, employees, satisfied customers, industry influentials, and others to *actively* advocate your brand or products to prospects. The tactics are "indirect" because the actual influencing of prospects is done by a third party and not by the company itself. Methods used to motivate these third parties include sales/trade incentives for distribution channel members, customer referral programs, endorsement and partnering arrangements, and others in which the goal is to have other individuals outside your company deliver positive messages that generate action among prospects.

Passive Direct Tactics

Passive direct tactics include all of the various tactics such as search engine marketing, directory listings, and point-of-purchase advertising described in *Level Three: Brand Visibility When and Where Desired*. These tactics are "direct" because it is the company itself rather than others communicating with prospects. However, it is "passive" on the company's part because prospects initiate the conversation or seek the information.

Passive Indirect Tactics

Passive indirect tactics are designed to ensure that current customers, respected authorities, distribution channel members, and other influentials know about your products and their advantages so that they can respond knowingly and positively when prospects seek their advice. The distinction between these "passive" indirect tactics and the "active" indirect tactics is that in this case the influentials are not being asked to actively promote the brand. Instead, the company's goal is more one of educating or giving information access to the influencers rather than incenting them to act.

The *primary* measurement of *Step 1* marketing communications activities among prospects should be the number/percentage and cost efficiency of getting prospects to take actions toward purchase or actually making a purchase.

The *secondary* measure for *Step 1* activities is the number/percentage and cost efficiency of prospects with whom the company communicated. The real value or return on investment to your company comes from prospects who take action toward purchase, not from simply delivering messages. That is why the resulting actions should be used as the primary measure of *Step 1* activities. Another useful *secondary* measure is the number/percentage of influencers actively advocating or helping to promote your brand.

Step 2. Make Initial Interaction Experiences Positive and Capture Critical Prospect Information

There are many ways in which interested prospects may respond or take action toward the purchase of your company's products. Some of those prospect actions are shown on the *Prospect Marketing Communications Chart*.

The second step is to ensure that the initial prospect interactions with your brand are as positive as possible for prospects and your company. As part of this step, most marketers should attempt to capture names, contact information, and other data from interested prospects. This information may be used to qualify prospects regarding their potential value to the company and/or likelihood of purchasing. And it will help you determine how much should be invested in converting the prospect into a customer.

PROSPECT MARKETING COMMUNICATIONS CHART

STEP 1

STRATEGY

Communications reaching out to potential prospects to provide reasons why they may be interested in the product or company and persuading them to

(a) Learn more.
(b) Try the product.
(c) Experience the brand.
(d) Take some other step toward purchase.

ACTIVITY

Active Direct Tactics
Communicate directly with the audience via
1. Advertising
2. Publicity
3. Sponsorships
4. Events
5. Other

Active Indirect Tactics
Encourage distribution channel members, employees, satisfied customers, and industry influentials to actively advocate your brand.

Passive Direct Tactics
Visibility when/where prospects are or go when they seek the product category. Includes search marketing, directory listings, and point-of-purchase advertising.

Passive Indirect Tactics
Ensure that customers, industry influentials, and distribution channel members are informed about your products and their advantages so they may respond appropriately when prospects seek their advice.

STEP 2

STRATEGY

Make the experience of these initial interactions as positive as possible for prospects and your company. Capture names, contact data, and other information from interested prospects. Enter qualified prospects in a marketing database.

ACTIVITY

Prospect Response Options
1. Contact company (call, response card, e-mail).
2. Visit Web site.
3. Visit/call dealer, store, or company representative.
4. Attend an event.
5. Consult a friend/expert.
6. Sign up for additional communications.
7. Purchase product.
8. Others.

STEP 3

STRATEGY

If no immediate purchase occurs, establish an ongoing dialogue designed to help the best prospects through the decision-making/purchase process. Continue to encourage prospects to take steps toward purchase.

ACTIVITY

Ongoing Dialogue With Qualified Prospects
Dialogue options include:
1. Direct mail
2. E-mail
3. Telephone
4. Fax
5. In-person contact
6. Wireless
7. Other

MEASUREMENT

Primary Measurement

1. Number/percentage of prospects taking actions toward purchase or making an actual purchase.

Secondary Measurement

1. Number and percentage of prospects with whom company communicated.
2. Number and percentage of influencers actively advocating your brand.

MEASUREMENT

Primary Measurement

1. Number/percentage of prospects taking additional actions toward purchase or making an actual purchase.

Secondary Measurement

1. Quantity and quality, as judged by prospects, of the communications delivered during the response phase.

MEASUREMENT

Primary Measurement

1. Number/percentage of prospects purchasing product.

Secondary Measurement

1. Number/percentage of prospects responding to specific marketing communications.

Purchase or No Purchase Decision

The chapter of this book describing *Actual Experiences With the Brand or Product* discussed some challenges and suggestions for making these initial experiences as positive as possible. See the discussion regarding *Investing in Initial Touch Points*. Capturing information from interested prospects into a database is essential for measuring the results for *Steps 1* through *3* and tying those results to your marketing communications activities. This also facilities the customization and personalization of ongoing communications for *Step 3* so that they will be more effective.

The *primary* measurement in *Step 2* should be the number/percentage and cost efficiency of interested prospects taking additional actions toward purchase or actually making a purchase. Ultimately, you must be able to determine what percentage of qualified interested prospects go on to make a purchase and what percentage fall out at various stages of the process. This enables you to determine the amount you can spend on various prospecting activities while delivering a satisfactory return on investment.

A *secondary* measure in *Step 2* is the quantity of communications and experiences delivered, as well as the quality of those communications and experiences, as judged by the prospects.

Step 3. Establish an Ongoing Dialogue

In many cases, it is desirable and/or necessary to engage in an ongoing dialogue with prospects. This depends upon the product, the prospects, and the purchase process. Big-ticket items are more likely to justify ongoing dialogue than products with minimal cost, unless they are purchased in large quantities. Qualified prospects representing significant potential revenue and/or with a good probability of purchasing are more likely to justify ongoing dialogue. And products with a typical multiple-week or -month purchase consideration process tend to require an ongoing dialogue. Of course, the goal is to help the best prospects through the decision-making process so that they ultimately become a customer.

The ongoing communications, sometimes referred to as "database," "relationship," or "lead conversion" marketing communications, may occur through various media. As shown on the *Prospect Marketing Communications Chart*, some of the possible vehicles include direct mail, e-mail, telephone, fax, in-person contact, and wireless communications.

It is important to realize that these ongoing communications may involve multiple individuals on the selling side and/or on the buying side of the dialogue rather than just being from the company to the prospect. On the seller side, the communications could come from marketing, technical, and service people within the company, as well as from dealers, distributors, or sale representatives outside the company. On the buying side, there could be multiple family members or several employees of a company involved in the decision making process.

The *primary* measure of *Step 3* activities is the number/percentage and cost efficiency of prospects that purchase the product or service. The key questions to answer for each communications tactic are:

1. Did more prospects buy the product or spend more with our company after engaging in the communications?
2. Does the long-term value, rather than just the immediate revenue, of the customers obtained more than offset the cost of the communications?

A *secondary* measure of *Step 3* activities is the number/percentage and cost efficiency of prospects responding to specific marketing communications.

CHAPTER **13**

Marketing Communications for Current Customer Audiences

Once someone becomes a customer of your company or brand, there is a change in the factors that influence her future purchases and your goals as a marketer. Comments from friends and other influentials, the right types of advertising and publicity, and other forms of marketing communications on the second through fourth levels of the *Hierarchy* may still have some impact on future purchases by current customers. However, that impact will be small compared to the customer's own experience with your product, brand, and company. That is why this customer experience represents the top level of the *Hierarchy of Marketing Communications Effectiveness*.

A company's marketing goals should be very different for current customers than for prospects. With prospects, the goals are focused on getting interested prospects to take initial steps toward purchase and converting those interested prospects to customers. Among customers, the primary focus needs to be on making the customer experience the best it can be, while still providing the company with a satisfactory margin. Additional goals among customers may include generating repeat purchases, higher volume purchases, accessory purchases, and trial of the company's other products, as well as advocating the brand and products to other individuals.

The *Customer Marketing Communications Chart* on page 74 reflects the goals that are unique to customers. This chart displays a two-tier continuous process. Whereas the process for any single *prospect* is linear in that the goal is to move them through the steps until a purchase is made, the process for an individual customer is continuous. Marketers should constantly be working to enhance the customer's experience and to maximize the asset value of the customer. For most companies, it is essential to have a good marketing database of customers in order to identify, learn about, and interact with customers in a personalized manner, as well as to measure the results of the communications activities.

Step 1. Deliver Exceptional Customer Experiences

At the top of the *Customer Marketing Communications Chart* is the need to deliver exceptional customer experiences, the importance of which has been emphasized in other chapters of this book. The challenge for marketing professionals is to explore ways in which marketing communications can enhance customer experiences rather than leaving this responsibility completely to Manufacturing, R & D, Customer Service, or Sales departments. The activities in this first step may be grouped into two categories:

1. Combine product quality, services, and communications to deliver superior customer experiences.
2. Enlist company employees, channel members, and other customers in delivering exceptional customer experiences.

Discussion of these two categories follows:

Combine Product Quality, Services, and Communications to Deliver Superior Customer Experiences

There are thousands of ways marketing communications can be used to help enhance the overall customer experience with your company and its products. Do not underestimate the importance to the overall customer experience of ongoing communications beginning with simple thank-you letters and continuing with other communications that deliver information and build the relationship. Marketing communications can add value to your products and enhance the experience of consumer or business customers by providing

1. Information
2. Entertainment

3. Convenience
4. Personalization
5. Commemoration
6. Community

Examples and ideas for enhancing the value of your products are covered in the third section of this book.

Enlist Company Employees, Channel Members, and Other Customers in Delivering Exceptional Customer Experiences

Customer interactions with your company's employees, channel members, such as dealers and distributors, and other customers are critical to the perceived quality of customer experiences. Employees and channel members that are positive, friendly, knowledgeable, helpful, and honest when interacting with customers contribute mightily to positive customer experiences. This is true during the purchase consideration phase, the actual purchase phase, immediate post-purchase phase, and ongoing customer service phase of the relationship. Positive interactions with other customers also enhance customer experiences.

Marketing communications that help encourage employees, channel members, and customers to be more positive, friendly, knowledgeable, helpful, and honest in dealing with customers (and prospects) make customer experiences better. These marketing communications will result in more sales of your products to customers and prospects as well. Marketing communications cannot make a basically unfriendly person friendly or a dishonest person honest. However, marketing communications that help train and educate employees and channel members regarding your products or strengthen relationships with your company will improve customer experiences.

Create and distribute printed, video, online, and wireless materials that help make employees, channel members, and current customers more knowledgeable regarding your products, better able to communicate product advantages, and more likely to provide superior service to customers. Develop ongoing communications materials and marketing programs that strengthen the relationship with the company and create more positive attitudes among all the individuals that interact with customers. Finally, monitor and improve automated voice, online, and other systems with which customers interact to ensure the experiences are the best they can be.

CUSTOMER MARKETING COMMUNICATIONS CHART

STEP 1

STRATEGY

Deliver an exceptional customer experience.

ACTIVITY

1. Combine product quality, services, and communications to deliver superior customer experiences.
2. Enlist company employees, channel members, and other customers in this effort.

STEP 2

STRATEGY

1. Identify individual customers and capture contact information, purchase activity data, preferences, satisfaction levels, potential value as a company asset, and other information in a marketing database.

2. Implement activities to increase asset value of customers and improve satisfaction levels.

ACTIVITY (based on level of customer satisfaction)

Very Positive (Promoter)

Direct your marketing dialogue to:

1. Maintain/increase satisfaction level by enhancing customer experience.
2. Keep customer informed regarding product/brand.
3. Encourage repeat/upgrade purchases.
4. Encourage to try/buy additional products/services.
5. Collaborate with customers to enhance products/services and develop new ones.
6. Encourage referrals/positive word-of-mouth communications.

Neutral (Passive)

Direct your marketing dialogue to:

1. Increase satisfaction levels by improving individual customer experiences.
2. Keep customers informed regarding product/brand.
3. Encourage repeat/upgrade purchases.
4. Encourage to try/buy additional products/services.
5. Collaborate with customers to enhance products/services and develop new ones.
6. Encourage referrals/positive word-of-mouth communications.

Negative (Detractor)

Direct your marketing activities to:

1. Fix problems and/or reduce dissatisfaction if possible.
2. Quarantine the negative effects.
3. Help customers to find a more satisfactory experience elsewhere

MEASUREMENT

Primary Measurement
1. Net Promoter Score or other customer satisfaction measures.

Secondary Measurement
1. Positive actions by employees, channel members, and customers.
2. Improvement in knowledge or opinions of employees, channel members, and customers regarding your company and products.

MEASUREMENT

Primary Measurement
1. Changes in asset value of customers—direct revenues through purchases plus indirect revenues through referrals and other activities.

Secondary Measurement
1. Number/percentage of customers taking actions towards purchase of additional products/services.
2. Changes in customer satisfaction levels.
3. Responses to and participation in customer experience-enhancing and asset-building activities.
4. Problems fixed.

DESIRED RESULTS
(From the Step 2 Activity)

1. Repeat purchase of current products at same or greater frequency.
2. Purchases accessory items.
3. Tries/purchases additional products/services.
4. Requests/seeks information regarding additional products/services (online/offline; from company, or channel partners).
5. Provides feedback to company to help improve/fix problems.
6. Collaborates with company to enhance current products/services or help develop new ones.
7. Reviews company-delivered communications and/or signs up to receive ongoing communications.
8. Participates in customer community/events.
9. Joins a customer club/group.
10. Actively advocates company/brand/products through referrals and other positive word-of-mouth communications.

The *primary* measurement of *Step 1* activities should be customer satisfaction levels. The Net Promoter Score (NPS) is one frequently used satisfaction measure that has been proven successful. It is easy to implement and has a track record of correlating with future company growth. It was discussed earlier in this book. Other measurement systems could be used as well.[1]

Regardless of the measurement system employed, it must provide the company with an ongoing measure of customer satisfaction. At the same time, it must encourage those who interact with customers to actually improve service levels and customer experiences, rather than encourage them to just receive higher satisfaction scores.

One *secondary* measurement of *Step 1* activities is the number and quality of positive actions taken by employees, channel members, and customers that may result in improved customer experiences. For example, you might measure the number of channel members that requested materials regarding your company's product, reviewed information online, or completed a training course.

Another *secondary* measurement of *Step 1* activities is improvement in knowledge or opinions of your company and its products among employees, channel members, and customers. Typically, this type of measurement could be made through a survey.

Step 2. Capture Individual Customer Information and Increase Asset Value of Customers

The second step is to increase the customers' asset value to your company. To do this, customers must be treated differently depending upon their satisfaction level. Further, the amount of company resources devoted to each customer should vary depending upon their asset value to the company. This requires your company to identify individual customers, at least the most valuable ones, and obtain critical information regarding them.

Ideally, information regarding satisfaction levels, customer potential for future purchasing and influencing others, product preferences, needs, and communications preferences should be collected and retained in a customer marketing database. Rather than attempting to collect all of the information at once, think of this as an ongoing dialogue in which you obtain information over time and use it to fine-tune your marketing communications.

The marketing communications activities and the emphasis you place on each should depend upon whether a particular customer is very satisfied, neutral/passive, or dissatisfied. As shown in the *Customer Marketing Communications Chart*, the recommended marketing communications activities are similar for very satisfied and neutral/passive customers. The difference is that most of the asset-building marketing communications activities are likely to produce greater results among customers that are very satisfied than among those who are neutral/passive. For neutral/passive customers, the most productive asset-building activities may be to determine why satisfaction levels are merely "OK" and seek ways to improve their customer experiences.

The customer asset-building marketing communications activities shown on the chart include communications intended to

1. Maintain and increase customer satisfaction.
2. Keep customers informed.
3. Encourage repeat/upgrade purchases.
4. Encourage trial/purchase of additional products/services.
5. Collaborate with customers to enhance and/or develop new products/services.
6. Encourage referrals/positive word-of-mouth communications.

Consider combining some of the following:

1. Marketing programs, such as frequent buyer programs, customer referral programs, and customer clubs.
2. Features such as online communities, customer events, and online/offline resources.
3. Standardized communications vehicles, such as printed or online newsletters, magazines, and catalogs.
4. Unique personalized targeted mail, e-mail, and other communications featuring announcements, opportunities, and offers.

The volume of and investment in these marketing communications activities delivered to customers should depend upon each customer's potential asset value to the company, as well as the customer's receptivity to each communications activity. It makes little sense to invest a lot of resources in marketing communications to those customers who are unable or unlikely to buy from the company again and unlikely to be in contact with prospective customers.

On the other hand, marketers should invest greater resources in customers that currently represent the most business, have potential to significantly increase their business with the company, or have great ability and potential to influence the purchases by other individuals. Therefore, it is important for your company to identify its Most Valuable Customers, Most Growable Customers, and Most Influential Customers and then devote greater resources to communicating with them.[2] This is the essence of customer database marketing communications strategy.

Potential positive customer actions based upon asset-building marketing communications are shown on the *Customer Marketing Communications Chart*. Any time customers take any of these actions, measurable marketing value has been delivered to your company.

Before discussing types of measurement, let's address those customers with negative opinions regarding your company or one of its products. Negative customer experiences have the potential to lower or end the future asset value of a customer. Ongoing communications with customers that encourage them to notify you of any dissatisfaction are essential to reducing this problem.

Among those customers with negative satisfaction levels, your company's focus should be on fixing the problem, reducing the dissatisfaction, and quarantining the negative effects as much as possible. In order to accomplish this, you must have a system for identifying individuals that are dissatisfied and be able to learn of negative customer experiences as soon as possible after they occur.

A good marketing communications system may be able to identify dissatisfied individuals and provide early detection of individual negative customer experiences. However, it is unlikely that marketing communications personnel or systems have the authority or ability to fix most problems. Thus, it is essential that marketing communications people and systems are well integrated with the people and systems that have the authority and ability to address the problems.

It is beyond the scope of this book to discuss systems and techniques for fixing problems and reducing dissatisfaction. However, we will take a moment to discuss the importance of quarantining dissatisfaction. There are two aspects of quarantining dissatisfaction.

The first aspect concerns customers that have historically been satisfied with your company but encounter a specific negative experience. What is critical in this situation is to (a) have an aggressive system to identify these negative experiences when they are happening or as soon as possible afterwards and (b) taking whatever steps are necessary to resolve the problems or make up for them before they destroy the overall relationship with the customer.

The second aspect of quarantining dissatisfaction is to do as much as possible to prevent or stop dissatisfied customers that are inclined to aggressively share their dissatisfaction with other people. The consequences of negative word-of-mouth communications can be far greater than that of positive word-of-mouth communications. Negative word-of-mouth has always been bad, but the Internet has made its potential impact more immediate and devastating.

Negative postings in online communities, forums, and blogs are common. Negative reviews on online stores, graphic videos on media such as You Tube, and creation of anti-company Web sites such as www.CompanyX Sucks.com can happen as well. Obviously, prevention is best. When prevention is not possible, companies need to have a strategy to combat or reduce the impact of negative actions.

It is easy to say that companies should strive to repair and address all customer problems and dissatisfactions. The reality is that it is most important to deal with those problems most likely to cause the greatest reduction in asset value for the company. This is another reason why it is important to identify those Most Valuable, Most Growable, and Most Influential Customers, uncover their problems, and resolve them.

The *primary* measurement used for *Step 2* communications activity is change in asset value of customers. To the extent possible, measure actual revenue from specific customers through purchases and measure indirect purchases those customers generate through referrals or other activities. Most companies will find it impossible to track 100 percent of these direct and indirect purchases because they are made through dealers or other intermediaries. Still, it is important to attempt to track as much of this activity as possible—especially among the most important customer groups.

Several types of *secondary* measures may be valuable in *Step 2*. These include

1. The number/percentage of customers taking actions toward the purchase of additional products/services.
2. Changes in customer satisfaction levels.
3. Responses to and participation in customer experience enhancing and asset-building activities.
4. Success rates in fixing or reducing customer problems.

Before leaving the discussion of the *Customer Marketing Communications Chart*, it is important to point out that at times part of the marketing communications process for customers will more closely follow the prospect process described earlier. When a company is attempting to cross-sell additional products or services to a current customer, the initial step will be to reach out to those customers having a potential interest and persuade them to learn more, try the product, or take some other step toward purchase. From there, the goal is to move customers through the prospect process toward purchase. This prospect process does not replace the customer marketing communications process, but instead occurs simultaneously as a part of the overall customer experience.

SECTION 3

IDEAS

Examples and Ideas for
Developing Marketing Communications
That Enhance the Value of Your Products

CHAPTER **14**

An Introduction to Marketing Communications-Based Product Value Enhancements

The first section of this book built the case for allocating more of your resources among the types of marketing communications efforts that are most trusted by audiences and are therefore, most likely to impact their purchase decisions. The second section offered suggested processes for developing effective, measurable marketing communications programs among your current and prospective customers. This third section is intended to help with the ambitious task of using marketing communications not just to communicate with your target audiences but to add value to your company's products as perceived by customers.

This section provides some examples of product-value-enhancing communications. However, it is as much about what could be done as it is about what has been done. These examples represent just the tip of the iceberg.

Our primary point in this section is that marketers have a tremendous opportunity to differentiate and increase the value of their products by adding enhancements to the products. Although product values may be increased by adding more features or services, product values also may be increased through the use of marketing communications.

The examples and suggestions in this book are just idea starters. As we mention several times, the possibilities of enhancing the value of products through marketing communications are limitless. Every day the invention and more widespread adoption of new media and new technologies expand the possibilities.

Our Advice

We offer two essential pieces of advice as you consider ways to use marketing communications to enhance the value of your products:

1. Be remarkable.
2. Think in terms of the customer rather than your company.

Small enhancements may be easier to implement and may add slight value to your product, but they will rarely translate into significant added value and sales. Unique, remarkable enhancements that cause customers to say "wow" and make them want to tell their friends about are the enhancements that are much more likely to yield the results you desire. Remarkable enhancements can be expensive to implement but do not have to be.

Realize that what it takes to add significant value to a product will vary depending upon the type and cost of the product. The value of low cost, frequently purchased products such as most food and beverages may be greatly enhanced by something fairly simple. On the other hand, it takes a lot more to significantly enhance the value of an automobile, boat, lawn mower, or computer.

It is critical to think in terms of what customers want and value rather than in terms of what is in your company's own self-interest. We have seen companies end up very disappointed in the results because they focused on trying to make customers more loyal to the company rather than adding real value for the customer. Creating a customer club or "loyalty" program with features limited to a company cap, membership certificate, and a periodic newsletter rarely produces great results.

We encourage you to get to know your customers, understand what would be of real value to them, be creative, and think in terms of big ideas. This is one place where a marketing communications agency that understands the audience, but can view the situation from a different perspective, can be of invaluable service.

Two Introductory Examples

Many marketers think of their products as little more than commodities. They believe there is little difference between their product and those of competitors. They may be right when it comes to the physical product alone. These marketers may hope to beat their competitors strictly on price, by having better distribution, or with a great advertising campaign. This is not to say that better distribution and great advertising cannot contribute mightily to a product's success. They can and do. Obviously, there will always be a portion of the market that simply wants to buy the lowest priced product in a category. However, it is important to look beyond distribution, advertising, and low price.

Consider two products that could easily be thought of as commodities: bubble gum and bottled water. The Topps Company began selling its Bazooka Bubble Gum shortly after the end of World War II. However, it was not until 1953 that Bazooka Bubble Gum began to separate itself from the competition. That is when the company added value-enhancing marketing communications to the product by including Bazooka Joe comics in the packages of gum. Suddenly, the package of gum became more distinctive and valuable because of the addition of the comics. The gum itself had not changed, but the value of the product increased because the total product experience improved. More recently, Topps has used the marketing communications tactic of inviting customers to vote on new members to be added to the Bazooka Joe Gang.[1]

For a current example of product differentiation and enhanced value through marketing communications, take a look at Australian bottled-water marketer iLove. What makes iLove stand out from all the other bottled waters? Attached to each bottle is a 32-page color glossy minimagazine. iLove found that in Australia the biggest-volume consumers of bottled water are women aged 14 to 35. So the minimagazine features a mix of celebrity gossip and fashion tips that are easily read on the go. Multiple versions of the magazine are published each month, so that there is reason to purchase multiple bottles. Yes, iLove does accept advertising in its minimagazine.[2]

These are just two examples of companies that have used marketing communications to enhance the value of their products. As you read the rest of this report and think about the possibilities for your company, do not limit yourself to the physical product itself. Think in terms of the customers' experiences with the product from the time of pre-purchase information gathering and purchase, to product set up, actual use, service, and other activities. Any of these may offer excellent opportunities to enhance the value of the product through marketing communications.

The examples and ideas presented in the next few chapters are all about delivering better *Actual Experiences With the Brand or Product*. That was Level One of our *Hierarchy of Marketing Communications Effectiveness* presented in the first section of this book. Additionally, you will find that implementing the ideas in this third section will improve the volume and impact of Level Two communications—*Recommendations From Trusted Sources.*

CHAPTER **15**

Revisiting the Concept of Product Value

We need a basic understanding of the concept of *product value* before we can discuss ways of increasing the value of products. A product, whether it is a bottle of water, a backpack, a computer, or some type of apparel has value only from the viewpoint of the buyer or user. Only the buyers or users can truly assign value to a product because they are the people willing to pay for it. To the buyer or user, a product is a combination of value satisfactions.

For example, a backpack is not simply a product in which to carry various items. Its value satisfactions go beyond that to include how comfortable it is to wear, its long-term durability, its ability to withstand the elements and to protect the items inside, its visual/sensory appeal, the image it conveys regarding the user, and many other satisfactions.

In addition, the value satisfactions for the backpack go beyond those associated with the physical product to include the buying process and acquisition of the product. The convenience and enjoyment of learning about the backpack, shopping for it, having questions answered, taking possession of it, and beginning to use it are some of those value satisfactions. While the backpack may be nearly ideal because of its size, comfort, compartments, and appearance, its value is diminished if you cannot easily find it in stores or on the Internet, if you must wait weeks for it to be delivered, or if the store sales clerk was rude and lacking in product knowledge. Additionally, extra features, services, information, or other enhancements you receive upon purchasing the product are among the value satisfactions. Obviously, the importance of various value satisfactions and the amount someone is willing to pay for them varies by individual and product.

The Total Product Concept

One of the most useful marketing ideas developed in the last 50 years is **The Total Product Concept** introduced by Theodore Levitt in the 1983 book, *The Marketing Imagination*. The Total Product Concept is illustrated below.[1]

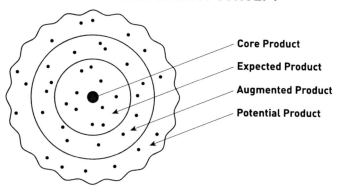

Note: The dots inside each ring represent specific activities or tangible attributes. For example, inside the "Expected Product" could be warranty, adequate packaging, a basic user's guide, access to parts and maintenance, and a basic company Web site.

The illustration above shows a series of concentric circles representing various types of attributes that, in total, make up an individual's perception of the value of a product.

The solid black area in the center represents the Core Product. This is the actual physical product.

Moving outward, the next area covers the Expected Product. It includes the Core Product plus the customer's minimal expectations of what is included with the Core Product. The Expected Product might include certain packaging, conveniences, basic services, standard guarantees, a toll-free customer service number, and other basics. These basic expectations must be met for an individual to even consider purchasing the product.

The next ring represents the Augmented Product. This is where true product differentiation begins. The value of the product may be enhanced by augmenting the Expected Product with additional services, conveniences, information, and other features that go beyond what is expected by the customer. Augmentations do not have to be completely new features. They may be significant improvements on Expected Product features. For example, assume that consumers expect a particular type of product to have a one-year warranty. The Augmented Product might have a three-year warranty. Augmentations may be absorbed into the basic price of the product or they may be offered for an added charge. Over time, some augmentations may come to be part of the consumer's Expected Product.

Finally, the last ring of the illustration represents the Potential Product. The Potential Product consists of the Core Product, Expected Product, and Augmented Product plus everything else that is potentially feasible to add now or in the future to attract and hold customers. Whereas the Augmented Product includes everything that has been or is being done, the Potential Product includes everything that could be done. Thus, the size and scope of the ring representing the Potential Product is limitless.

Let's use a basic cup of coffee to illustrate the principles of the Total Product Concept. Start with the Core Product: a basic cup of coffee in some type of container. Millions of places in the United States, ranging from vending machines and convenience stores to specialty coffee shops and bookstores, offer a basic cup of coffee. For decades, most consumers' Expected Product for a cup of coffee included being able to get various cup sizes, regular versus decaf, and an insulated cup holder. At some point, specialty coffee retailers such as Starbucks began to offer various blends and flavors of coffees, espresso and latte options, and other enhancements. At one time, these were part of the Augmented Product but now have become part of the Expected Product when it comes to Starbucks and other specialty coffee retailers.

Consider some other augmentations that Starbucks has offered. Starbucks has made their product more convenient to find, not only by opening thousands of stand-alone stores but also by making their product available in bookstores, shopping malls, airports, and even Bass Pro Shops stores. Other augmentations include very pleasant surroundings and a chance to try new coffee blends and varieties.

What happens when the server at the Starbucks store forgets to make your beverage or takes too long to do so? For most customers, the Expected Product in this situation might be a simple apology for the neglect or slow service. (Sadly, at the retail stores of many companies, this expectation would not be met.) However, at our local Starbucks the above situation has been handled on more than one occasion not just with a sincere apology but also with a card for a free beverage on our next visit.

And what would a cup of coffee be without high-speed Internet access? A few years ago, someone was thinking about the Potential Product when they decided to offer Wi-Fi access at their coffee shop. What was a Potential Product has become the Augmented Product and is moving toward becoming part of the Expected Product.

More and more marketers are thinking beyond the purely technical product features and standard services associated with the Core and Expected Products to enhance the value satisfactions they deliver to consumers. Oakley's Bluetooth-enabled eyewear and the Nike + iPod Sports Kit, which measures and records the distance and pace of a walk or run, are examples. In fact, the entire Nike + iPod experience is an excellent example of expanding into the Potential Product.

Physical product enhancements and extra services represent two outstanding types of augmentations available to marketers. However, there is a third source of potential augmentations that can increase the value of your products: **marketing communications**. That is the focus of the next chapters.

CHAPTER **16**

The Scope of Marketing Communications

The term *marketing communications* has different definitions for different individuals. Some people think of marketing communications as synonymous with advertising. Others may expand the scope to include sales literature, catalogs, and some other common tools.

We have a much broader perspective of marketing communications. We define marketing communications as all activities involved in delivering messages to and receiving messages from a target audience, regardless of the media or method used. Marketing communications includes not only advertising and sales literature but also activities such as public relations, sales promotion, database marketing communications, telemarketing, events, point-of-purchase materials, package design, and word-of-mouth communications. Also, marketing communications includes newer media and tools such as Web sites, e-mail, blogs, search engine marketing, and podcasts.

Marketing communications consist of activities designed to send and receive messages with all types of audiences, including end users, influencers, dealers, and other members of distribution channels, internal company personnel, and the media. Taking a broad perspective of marketing communications enables us to uncover many opportunities to use it to enhance the value of products, much in the same way that it helps to think about products in terms of the Total Product Concept.

Advertising as a Value Enhancer?

The next several chapters of this book suggest how various forms of marketing communications could be used to enhance the value of products. However, before we address this, we should touch upon whether the most well-known marketing communications tool, media advertising, enhances the value of products.

Some people argue that advertisements appearing in magazines, television, and other media make consumers aware of products and their benefits but do not add actual value to the product itself. After all, the advertisements are available to everyone, both customers and noncustomers, so they are not really adding value to the products for people who buy them. On the other hand, some individuals argue that by communicating a product image, advertising can enhance the value of the product. Thus, a product perceived via advertising as having a better image or as having an image more consistent with the image a customer desires may be perceived as having greater value.

In this book, we choose to deal with the question of whether advertising can add value to products in a simple way by avoiding the issue. We avoid the issue not because it lacks merit, but because it interferes with the key point we want to make. That point is how marketers can creatively use marketing communications to add actual **tangible** value to their products. We want to explore some of the ways in which various marketing communications tools can provide product augmentations.

We will not attempt to address all of the possible ways in which marketing communications can enhance the value of products. Those ways are limitless and are continuously growing as new media and marketing communications tools are developed. Instead, we will provide some examples of opportunities to use marketing communications to enhance product value. Hopefully, these examples will serve as thought starters for your own unique situation.

CHAPTER **17**

How Marketing Communications Can Add Value to Products

When considering product value, it is important to think of the Total Product Concept as described in Chapter 15. Likewise, it is essential to think in terms of the customers' product experiences. For customers, a big part of the value of most products is the experience they have with the products. For example, a fishing boat is not just a device that floats in the water and allows an angler to catch fish. It is a tool that enables an angler to relax and have fun with friends and family while fishing. Anything the boat does or has that enhances that total experience increases its value. Anything about the boat that detracts from that experience, even if it has nothing to do with the core part of the boat, decreases its value.

The product experience is not limited solely to the time spent actually using the product. Product experience includes learning about the product, purchasing it, taking delivery of it, preparing to use it, having it repaired or serviced, showing it to friends, and any other interactions the customer has with the product, the company, distribution channels, or service people.

There are at least six key ways in which marketing communications can enhance the product experience and add value to products. These six ways are

1. **Information**
2. **Entertainment**

3. Convenience
4. Personalization
5. Commemoration
6. Community

We will briefly discuss each of these six potential value enhancers.

Information

Information may offer the most potential for value enhancement by marketing communications. Anything that helps customers to more effectively use a product or discover more opportunities to use a product enhances the product value. However, the value of information does not stop there. Information that enables the customer to be more knowledgeable regarding the activities or context in which the product is used, to impress friends or family, or to have a greater feeling of affinity or closeness to the product or brand can add to the value.

Entertainment

People like to be entertained. Marketing communications can amuse, energize, charm, captivate, inspire, intrigue, dazzle, or delight customers. When used in this manner, it can add value to products. The Bazooka Joe comics are an example of this.

Convenience

Consumers are starved for time more than ever before. Often they would like to spend more time enjoying their favorite pursuits and less time completing necessary, but less enjoyable, tasks. Time is a precious resource. Value is added when marketing communications makes it easier for the enthusiast to participate in his or her favorite activities or reduce the time required to complete less desirable tasks.

Personalization

Marketing communications that help customers to customize or personalize the product experience for themselves add value to the product. Many customers will benefit from being able to customize the product to meet their own needs and preferences. If a company personalizes its interactions or services for the individual customer in a beneficial way, this adds value to the product experience.

Commemoration

Many activities are not just valued for the immediate experience. Part of the joy is in being able to relive or recount the experience for yourself or for friends and family. "Life caching," as Trendwatching.com refers to it, is the growing desire among consumers to collect and store possessions, memories, and experiences in order to create personal histories and mementos of their lives or to relive an experience at a later time. Marketing communications that facilitate "life caching" or commemorating great experiences adds value to the products.

Community

It is important to some individuals to have a sense of belonging. For others, being part of a community is beneficial because it gives them access to exclusive information or the opportunity to participate in activities they might otherwise not experience. Products, and the companies that market them, can contribute to this sense of belonging or community. Marketers can provide community by organizing events, facilitating communications among customers, providing exclusive materials, and encouraging other shared experiences in which the product plays a role.

Keep in mind that the goal should be to add something of significance when using marketing communications to enhance the value of a product. A good litmus test is whether the enhancement is so impressive that a customer would actively show it to friends or tell friends about it. An enhancement that merely provides a tidbit of information or a brief chuckle may be nice but will not add much value in the customer's mind. A feature worth telling others about is a true value-added enhancement.

CHAPTER **18**

Marketing Communications Ideas to Enhance the Value of Products

This chapter of the book introduces some ideas and considerations for using various marketing communications tools to enhance the value of products. We will explore the following marketing communications tools:

1. Packaging
2. Product Manuals/User Guides
3. Catalogs
4. Web Sites and Other Internet Tools
5. Alerts/Reminders/Updates
6. Mobile/Wireless Applications
7. Magazines/Newsletters
8. Events
9. User Groups/Customer Clubs

Packaging

When manufacturers think about product packaging, the focus is typically on its role in protecting the product from the environment and its role in helping to sell the product in the store. Packaging helps to sell the product by attracting attention, identifying the contents, and communicating the brand message and product attributes. These are essential roles for packaging. However, there are other ways packaging can add value for the customer or prospective customer.

As a means of generating ideas for packaging to enhance the value of your products, for example, ask the following questions:

1. Does the package add to the customer's convenience, help to transport the product, or improve storage of the product when not in use?

2. Can the customer utilize the package post-sale to display the product, provide important information, or offer some other utility rather than simply being thrown away?

3. Is it easy and convenient to quickly open the package in order to access and use the product? (This could be important for products that may need to be used at a moment's notice.)

4. Does the outside or inside of the package contain information that makes the product easier to assemble or use? (As many products become more technically advanced, they have greater appeal. But they may frighten potential customers who believe they lack the technical skills to properly use the product. Packaging that conveys information and offers assistance in this area may lessen these fears.)

5. Does the packaging contain information that may help the customer to become more proficient in using the product or find additional uses for the product? (Many food product manufacturers accomplish this by printing recipes on or within the packaging.)

6. Does the package contain information, offers, or discounts for accessories, add-on services, or something else that can enhance the customer's experience?

7. Does the package contain an entertaining, informative, or useful premium or bonus that would be of interest and

value to customers? (Remember Bazooka Joe comics or the iLove bottled water minimagazine.)

8. Does the package contain the address of a Web site with special services, information, entertainment, or other content of interest?

9. Does the outside of the package contain a special phone number or Web site address that potential customers can access via a cell phone or other mobile device that will provide more information to assist them in their buying decision?

Product Manuals/User Guides

A "good" product manual is one that clearly and quickly explains the basics of using a product, provides additional information regarding advanced features, and serves as a handy reference for troubleshooting or questions. A "great" product manual would go beyond this to provide even more valuable information, to entertain, or to make the customer feel very special about having purchased the product.

Some products are intended to be used as part of activities that give users a thrilling experience, a sense of accomplishment, an opportunity to commune with nature, the chance to spend quality time with loved ones, or to have fun. What is to prevent a product manual or a supplement to it from generating some of these feelings? Why can't a product manual be humorous, entertaining, exciting, beautiful, emotionally appealing, or very special in some other way? Can you include quotes or testimonials from customers or their kids telling how their lives were enhanced by spending time with family, enjoying nature, or solving a problem while using your product?

One of the best benefits a user guide can provide is to very quickly help new customers configure and begin using the product. If that first pleasurable experience with the product comes quickly and effortlessly, it enhances the value of the product. Software developer company Electric Rain has the right philosophy in designing user guides when they have the requirement that "the user has to be able to do something cool within 30 minutes of opening the guide."[1]

Keep in mind that product manuals/user guides do not have to be limited to a simple printed format. Consider supplementing printed material by using video, the Internet, or a DVD to provide visuals, animations, and demonstrations of steps or techniques described in the printed manual. These multimedia tools may be even more impactful in showcasing some of the ideas described in the paragraphs above.

The importance and value of an enhanced product manual will depend upon the type of product and its cost. Obviously, a manual that costs $10 per copy to produce would not make economic sense for many products. However, for those products requiring extensive instructions for use, the goal should be to transform the basic product manual from something that the new customer must "get through" prior to using the product into something so good that the customer will want to show family or friends.

Catalogs

Many manufacturers' catalogs are thought of primarily as tools to present the company's range of products to consumers and dealers. Generally, a catalog is designed to convince the audience to buy a product and help them select the best product to meet their needs among several choices. Thus, the primary value of the catalog is to assist prospective customers before they buy the product rather than to benefit customers after the purchase.

That is not to say that catalogs do not provide anything of interest to customers. Some catalogs feature a variety of accessories or complementary products for purchase that can enhance the performance, comfort, convenience, uses, or other characteristics of the product that was purchased. Some catalogs contain charts, data, tips, or articles that can improve the customer's experience with the product. This type of content in a catalog certainly has the ability to enhance the value of the product for customers. The amount of the enhanced value typically ranges from very little to moderate, depending upon what content is included.

The primary concern many marketers are likely to have with enhancing their product catalog is cost. For many companies, the cost of creating, printing, and distributing the company's catalog(s) is huge. Often it is one of the largest line items in the marketing department's budget. The concern with adding value enhancements is that they will add more pages and more cost in a situation where most marketers are working hard to condense content and limit pages. So why add more content, more pages, and more cost to a tool whose primary role is to help prospective customers choose the right product and generate initial sales?

The answer to this concern is to think creatively and look for ways to enhance the catalog's value to the customer without adding significantly to the space and cost. One option is to think of the customer's experience with the catalog as not being confined to just the printed pages of the catalog. Icons, code numbers, barcodes, telephone numbers, URLs, or other items included as part of the product listings in the catalog pages can provide a door to an extra level of information, instruction, entertainment, or customization that is exclusive to customers that have purchased and registered a product.

Customers might access demonstration videos to help them set up, install, or use the product under varying conditions. If your company has an advisory staff or well-known company president, customers could view their comments and/or videos of them using the product. Perhaps customers can access a community of other users of the product to share tips, swap stories, receive advice, or arrange a get-together. Another possibility is to allow customers to provide you with feedback regarding the product, ask a question, suggest improvements, or offer ideas for additional uses.

Later in this chapter, we will discuss services that enable camera phone users to snap a photo of a barcode or a graphic on a product's package or on the product itself. That image captured by the camera phone enables the user to receive additional product information or other content via the phone. The same principle could be applied to a company's catalog where special codes, text, or icons could be printed that enable customers to access more product information, entertainment, instruction, or other material. Of course, the same thing could be accomplished by allowing customers to dial a dedicated telephone number or to text message a specific code.

A second, more traditional option is to think in terms of adding bound or inserted supplements only to those copies of your catalogs that are provided to customers once they purchase a product. These supplements may be printed material or something else, such as a DVD.

Another approach is to encourage customers to identify themselves to your company with the promise that they will receive a special edition of the catalog that not only describes the many available complimentary and accessory products but also has bonus material to enhance their experience with the product. This strategy has the potential to spur sales of accessories and other products, as well as add value to the product already purchased.

The opportunities for supplemental material are endless. As suggested earlier, think in terms of information, entertainment, convenience, personalization, commemoration, and community. Charts and data are possibilities. So is background information regarding how a product was developed or stories of unique customer experiences with the product. Other options include special software enabling customers to improve their experience with the product, record their adventures, or play games related to your product.

The key point with all of the above ideas is that there are many ways to enhance the utility and value of the catalog for customers without adding significantly to the printed pages. This is important if your catalog is a tool whose primary use is by prospective customers before they purchase. Increasing the utility of the catalog, as it relates to the product, increases the value of that product. Also, increasing the utility of the catalog encourages customers to spend more time with it, thus giving them more opportunities to discover and purchase other products your company offers.

Web Sites and Other Internet Tools

Web sites, e-mail, and other Internet applications offer marketers tremendous opportunities to add value to their products and brands through marketing communications. As the Internet expands in terms of users, capabilities, and capacity, these opportunities will continue to grow. Today marketers are held back from maximizing the potential of the Internet much more by a lack of imagination, ideas, and understanding of the customer than they are by limitations of technology or capacity.

Consider many manufacturer company Web sites. Often they are a collection of pages or images from the company's catalog, additional printed literature, and some other content regarding the company. This static material may be enhanced by close up or multi-dimensional product views, additional product details, lists of optional features, and a dealer locator. Finally, visitors to the site may be encouraged to "interact" with the company by sending an e-mail message to ask questions, signing up for e-mail updates, or completing a form to request product literature.

There is nothing wrong with the Web site as just described. It is what is expected by most consumers. However, because it is merely what is expected, it does not enhance the value of the product and does not add to the reasons why an individual would do business with the company. Further, if all the content and features on the Web site are accessible to everyone, there is no enhanced value given to someone for being a customer.

Think about the six types of value enhancers discussed earlier and how they could be used to strengthen your company's Web site to enhance the customer's experience. A few ideas are presented in the following paragraphs.

The first value enhancer is **information**. Many Web sites provide good information regarding each of the company's products, but often that is where the information stops. More advanced Web sites may offer some of the following:

1. Product selection advice or features.
2. Articles or videos with more information regarding products or techniques.
3. Ideas for more frequent product usage or enhanced user experiences with the product.
4. Information or resources related to the activities, occasions, situations, or conditions in which the product is likely to be used.

Web sites provide an opportunity for marketers to offer valuable information that is accessible only to customers.

1. If your company has a pro staff, in-house advisors, celebrity endorsers, or company ambassadors, can these people provide tips or other information that you make accessible only to customers?
2. Can you provide customers with a special e-mail address to ask questions or exclusive access to a database of valuable information?
3. Can you provide customers with unbiased, expert advice regarding related product categories in which your company does not compete (i.e., a lawn mower manufacturer could provide recommendations regarding sprinkler systems, gardening tools, or fertilizers)?

The second value enhancer is **entertainment**. Is there music, humor, action, drama, competition, games, challenges, or other entertainment you can make available exclusively to your customers via your Web site? There are many options for obtaining or developing such entertainment. Your company could create it if you have the talent, resources, and time to do so. You can have outside suppliers, such as an entertainment company, marketing agency, or freelancer, create it. Or you can purchase existing entertainment.

One other option for obtaining entertainment is to encourage your customers to create and provide the entertainment by submitting their own stories, photos, videos, etc. This option has the additional advantage of creating **community**, one of the other six value enhancers. If your company has community building events, such as rallies or other events with an entertainment component, can you give customers that cannot attend the live event an opportunity to view some of the activities via your Web site?

The third value enhancer, **convenience**, has great potential via the Internet. Customers that cannot attend distant events, training academies, or other in-person activities may be given virtual access or simulations of the experience through a Web site.

Obviously, Web sites can offer convenience by enabling customers to access product information and to purchase products without having to visit a store. Likewise, Web sites can help customers by organizing information and other resources for their convenience. This may include information regarding product use, regulations, available places to enjoy a particular activity, safety tips, recipes, or other types of information. Anything that saves customers time in finding information they seek or in accomplishing a necessary task has the potential to add value.

Convenience may be offered to customers in the form of reminders or automatic replenishments of products. Reminder systems are often based on a combination of information that is publicly available, proprietary to the company, and supplied by the customer. Customers can be reminded about anything ranging from the approach of a time when your product should be used, to product care and maintenance that needs to be done, to a friend's birthday.

The fourth value enhancer, **personalization**, is well known with Web sites. Features such as My Yahoo!, MySpace, and Amazon.com's personalized Web pages and e-mail are very popular and well known to most marketers. It is not difficult for a company to enable customers to establish their own personalized pages. Such pages could allow customers to highlight specific content of interest, maintain inventories of products owned or desired, list links to other Web sites of interest, and receive product recommendations or news based on personal preferences. The possibilities are limited not by the technology but by the imaginations of marketers. Personalization offers tremendous potential especially when paired with two of the other value enhancers, **commemoration** and **community**, which are discussed in the following paragraphs.

Many people have a strong desire to **commemorate** their accomplishments, adventures, and experiences. For some that may mean taking photos or video of the spectacular scenery they witnessed or the people they met. For others it may be the accomplishment of catching the "big one" while fishing, achieving a level of proficiency, or completing a do-it-yourself task around the house. Still others may want to remember quality time spent with a family member or new friendships developed while attending an event.

The desire and trend to record and commemorate important or pleasurable events has been referred to as "life caching." Marketers can add great value to their products and customer relationships by helping customers capture, retain, organize, and share with others (community) their important moments. These moments may be captured in the form of words, sounds, photos, or videos. All are not only possible on the Internet, they are being done. The Harley Davidson Photo Center is an excellent example of this type of site and service.

The sixth value enhancer, **community**, can come to life on a Web site when a company enables people to share opinions, experiences, or information with other enthusiasts or solution seekers via online forums and other means. Customers can establish or maintain relationships online. Also, Web sites can facilitate community when customers can post descriptions, photos, videos, or other content from community-enhancing events such as customer rallies.

Outdoor recreation marketers Cabelas', Bass Pro Shops, and REI demonstrate some of what is possible in terms of value enhancement, while at the same time allowing us to imagine even greater possibilities. Cabelas', Bass Pro Shops, REI, and others have turned the basic outdoor recreation retail store into something much greater. For many people, these stores are major travel destinations. Often they represent visits customers greatly anticipate. In addition to a huge selection of products, these stores are sensory and participatory masterpieces featuring displays, aquariums, practice ranges, climbing walls, product demonstrations, seminars, and much more. Many of the stores include family restaurants, ice cream stands, Starbucks coffee stands, and other services. No doubt new attractions will be added over time.

Now think about the Web sites for Cabelas', Bass Pro Shops, and REI. Each company has an excellent Web site offering customers good information and the convenience of online shopping. Further, these companies have done much on their Web sites to enhance the customer experience. In fact, a 2006 Cisco Systems study of retail Web sites in a variety of industries ranked the Cabelas' site at the very top, along with Amazon.com. The REI site was also among the top sites, while Bass Pro Shops was not included in the study.[2] Cabelas' Web site has many excellent extras, including a variety of product videos, buyers' guides, comparison charts, field guides, talk forums, photo-sharing services, video tours of retail stores, state-by-state recreation information, and more.

However, as outstanding as the Cabelas', Bass Pro Shops, and REI Web sites are, they still do not capture the magic that visits to the physical stores do. Perhaps they never will. Still, there is the potential to do so much more on these Web sites so that they go from being sites that people visit primarily when they want to buy something to sites people want to visit regularly because of the pleasure and interest the sites deliver. If companies can get people to visit their Web sites even when they are not actively seeking information or planning to buy products, the sites will undoubtedly generate unplanned purchases. The challenge is to maintain the current convenient shopping experience and solid information but go further so that the sites become "eagerly anticipated experiences" and weekly or daily destinations for enthusiasts.

Alerts/Reminders/Updates

Are there developments, updates, news, or other information related to your product or to the occasions in which it is used that should be shared with product users? Is there periodic maintenance, cleaning, or other care that should be performed at certain times of the year? Could customers benefit from being reminded several weeks in advance that a particular season, situation, or other opportunity to use your product will soon arrive? Are there local, regional, or national opportunities for customers to use your product, gather with other enthusiasts or solution seekers, or preview new products to which you can alert them? Are there special discounts, sales, or other buying opportunities customers would like to be informed about?

If any of the opportunities exist, you may be able to add value to your products by establishing an alert/reminder/update service for customers. Customers can participate in your marketing communications program by having them tell you what categories of alerts/reminders/updates they wish to receive, how they wish to receive them, and even when they wish to receive them.

The most obvious method for customers to request alerts and to specify preferences is via your Web site. Then they can receive e-mail notifications. This is likely to be the least costly approach, but there are challenges with ensuring that e-mail messages get through to recipients. Other communications options for specifying preferences and receiving alerts include telephone, regular mail, text messaging, and even fax. Thus, customers could visit a Web site to establish their preferences but receive messages via their cell phones or regular mail.

There are several well-known examples of customer alerts. Southwest Airlines has their DING service that delivers news of discount fares to the computers of subscribing customers. Amazon.com sends e-mail notices to customers whenever a new book is available that matches a customer's subject or author preferences. Of course, there are many news alert services, including those offered by Google, Info Beat, ESPN, and many online stock services.

Mobile/Wireless Applications

We have arrived at the era of Total Access. Consumers want access to information and services not only whenever they want them but also from wherever they are. The Internet gave consumers the potential, and now the expectation, for 24/7 access from their computers. Cell phones, PDAs, iPods, and other mobile devices offer the potential for access anywhere and anytime.

A good starting point for understanding the potential for mobile/wireless is with GPS manufacturer Trimble and their www.trimbleoutdoors.com Web site. Campers, hikers, anglers, hunters, and other outdoor-recreation enthusiasts can plan and create trips; download trips to a GPS receiver, BlackBerry, or GPS cell phone; use a GPS cell phone for route navigation and tracking; personalize and commemorate trips with photos taken by a camera phone; and share trips with friends and family. Customers can also research trips posted by other community members. Similarly, TrailRunner's route-planning software (www.trailrunnerx.com) offers a hint of what is possible using an iPod.

Think about your own company and its products. What information of value can you make available to customers via their cell phones when and where they want it? What audio or video content can be made available exclusively to customers via podcast downloads to their iPods, BlackBerrys, or other devices? Can your company add value to its products by offering a series of how-to features, monthly informational podcasts, or entertaining programming that can be downloaded to and/or accessed through wireless devices? Would this differentiate your products from those of competitors? Would this help attract interest from tech-savvy younger audiences new to your product category?

Camera features of cell phones offer another intriguing opportunity for marketers to add value through marketing communications and to differentiate themselves. Services such as Mobot, qode, and others allow individuals to snap a photo of a picture, barcode, phrase, or other element with their camera phone to access text, data, videos, or other content through the cell phone. This technology offers exciting possibilities for marketing communications to prospects that are considering your product and to customers after they purchase it.

Prospects in a store could snap a photo of a barcode or other image on the outside of the product package to access features/benefits, comparison data, or a video demonstration that would help them choose your product. For customers that have purchased the product, pages in the user guide, other information inside the package, or codes on the product itself can provide camera phone access to information of value.

Have a product that is challenging to set up or begin using? Include an image that enables new customers to see a step-by-step video or instructions. Snap a shot of an image or code on a canoe, portable generator, automobile jack, or other product to obtain access to tips for using these products under varying conditions or in a variety of situations.

Have a low-tech, inexpensive, frequently purchased product for which technical information is not an issue? Enhance the value for your customers and differentiate your product from competitors by including something inside the package that links a camera phone to entertaining video, music, jokes, or other content they would enjoy. Think of it as the cell phone equivalent of the Bazooka Joe comics or iLove minimagazine.

Magazines/Newsletters

Customer magazines and newsletters are two of the oldest marketing communications tools for enhancing the value of a product or relationship with customers. Many of these publications have been low-cost, very mediocre efforts that add only marginal value to the product in the customer's mind. More often they are tools of value to the company in its attempts to cross-sell other products, accessories, or services. There is nothing wrong with companies sending customers magazines, newsletters, or other materials with a focus on cross-selling. However, it is important for companies not to delude themselves into thinking that such communications will be perceived as greatly enhancing the value of an already-purchased product.

Marketers use various strategies when publishing company magazines and newsletters. Some publications are intended only for current owners of the company's products. Examples include Winnebago's *Traveling Times* magazine and Fleetwood's *Fleetwood Flyer* magazine. These publications add value to owning the companies' recreational vehicles by helping owners get more pleasure from using the products and giving them more involvement in the community of owners. Further, these publications support dialogue between owners and the company. Also, they give customers an opportunity to participate in what the company is doing.

Other companies publish magazines as a tool to spread the company or brand name and image among a wider audience. Examples include *Cabela's Outfitters Journal* and *Mossy Oak's Hunting the Country*. These magazines generate newsstand sales and are distributed in other ways. The magazines certainly create awareness for the companies and their products, spread the companies' images, and even generate income. However, they may not necessarily be perceived as added benefits of being customers of the companies because the magazines are available at newsstands to anyone. Still, to the extent that they are providing customers with greater knowledge and understanding of their products or showing them how to better use their products, these magazines may be enhancing the value of the products or brand experience.

A company magazine or newsletter is most likely to be perceived as significantly enhancing the value of a low-cost, frequently purchased product, where there is little perceived difference between brands. A magazine or newsletter by itself may not contribute significant additional value to big-ticket products unless the publication is one element of a major effort that helps define the total user experience. That is the case with the Winnebago and Fleetwood magazines. It is also the case with Harley Davidson publications *Enthusiast* and *HOG Tales*, which are part of the entire Harley Owners' Group package.

Events

The possibilities and opportunities to enhance product value for customers through events are limitless. Events can be local, regional, national, or international in scope. They can be organized and hosted by the national manufacturer, regional managers, individual dealers, end-user customers, or a combination of these groups. Events can be conducted in partnership with other companies' marketing-related or complementary products. They can be stand-alone events or tied to other major events.

Small-scale events give customers, and often prospective customers, an opportunity to try some products, receive instruction, enhance their knowledge, meet celebrities, participate in competitions, win prizes, enjoy the company of fellow enthusiasts, be entertained, raise money for a good cause, or some combination of these experiences. Bigger events may offer many of the same experiences, although on a grander scale. They can represent unique, once-in-a-lifetime adventures or annual events to which customers look forward. When well done, such events become a major part of the value people receive by being customers. In some cases, the events may have greater value to customers than the actual products.

Some companies already organize and host a variety of events. These range from owners' tournaments held by several fishing and boat companies to owners' rallies organized by RV companies, boat companies, and auto manufacturers, to special events at wineries. Many of these events are supported and enhanced by printed or online materials such as newsletters, articles in company magazines, photos, and discussion forums. Video is likely to play an increasing role as companies work to extend and enhance these experiences.

The North Face developed a unique event experience in which customers could participate when they sponsored ultramarathon runner Dean Karnazes in a series of 50 marathon races across the country. The North Face arranged for its customers to have an opportunity to run alongside Dean Karnazes during marathon races in customers' local areas.

One of the great examples of an event that enhances the value of the products for its customers is Camp Jeep. Jeep owners and their guests pay approximately $400 to attend the annual Camp Jeep event. The event is typically three days of concerts, classes, and various experiences.

Jeep 101 Village contains custom off-road courses to learn and improve customers' driving skills and displays showcasing new Jeep models. In the Engineering Village, Jeep owners get to hear from and provide suggestions to Jeep engineers.

The Sports and Adventure Village enables owners to participate in scuba diving, fly fishing, scavenger hunts, photography lessons, and other activities. Other villages feature kids' events, music, and a Jeep museum. Still other villages allow owners to receive maintenance tips, learn woodcarving, enjoy massages, and much more.

Camp Jeep is the type of event that creates customers for life while also giving owners an experience that they will communicate to their friends. Admissions cover part of the cost of Camp Jeep. Some other costs are covered by sponsorship fees paid by other companies excited to have the opportunity to interact with an enthusiastic group of active, upscale individuals.

Jeep also holds a series of Jeep Jamborees each year at various locations throughout the country. These events typically consist of a series of trail drives, group meals, and social activities. As with Camp Jeep, owners pay a fee to participate.[3]

Owners' Groups/Customer Clubs

Customer clubs and owners' groups can represent a tremendous enhancement that adds significant value to your product. Or they can be weak efforts that are at best neutral and could even damage the perception of your products. While they consist of more than just communications, marketing communications are a critical aspect of how valuable and successful they are. To begin, we will discuss weak customer clubs and owners' groups.

Poorly designed customer clubs and owners' groups are the ones that are set up primarily to benefit the company by collecting a customer name/address/e-mail so the company will have the opportunity to send messages hawking the company's products. These clubs usually amount to little more than a club name, an occasional newsletter, a trinket with the company logo, a certificate, or a membership card. Now with the Internet, club members may have access to a forum or chat area on the company's Web site. Perhaps, customers even receive the "privilege" of buying some of the company's logo merchandise. The bottom line is that these clubs are very one-sided to the benefit of the company.

The type of customer club described above may obtain some "members" if there is no cost to join. However, these customers are not likely to be avid members and they will not view such a club as enhancing the value of the product or strengthening their relationship with the company. The danger is that such a weak effort may reduce the perceived value of your product when customers compare your club with those of competitors or with clubs with which they are familiar.

Successful customer clubs and owners' groups are ones that offer members significant value and benefits, especially ones they cannot obtain anywhere else. Customer clubs and owners' groups that enhance the value of a product are likely to have several of the following characteristics and features:

1. Financial benefits that enable customers to purchase desirable products and services at deeply reduced prices or that significantly reward customers for regularly doing business with your company.
2. Access to special information, products, or services that are unavailable to nonmembers. Often this includes advance previews of new products and services as well as an opportunity to comment on them.
3. Opportunities to attend or participate in member-only events and activities at a convenient location and time. Ideally, there should be both local and national events and activities.
4. Opportunities to converse and build meaningful relationships with other members.
5. Access to key company management, product developers, and other personnel along with the ability to express opinions and contribute ideas.

6. An overall feeling of having special status and being viewed as special by friends/acquaintances as a result of being a member.

Great customer clubs and owners' groups increase the value of products by packaging together several different enhancements into a special bundle. The Harley Owners' Group (HOG) is a wonderful example. Marketing communications plays a major role in making successful clubs valuable to customers and to the company.

CHAPTER **19**

Measuring and Evaluating the Success of Marketing Communications-Oriented Product Enhancements

Let us assume that you have developed ideas for one or more product enhancements based on marketing communications. You are faced with two key questions. How do you know if this enhancement will be successful? How do you measure the success of the enhancement once it is implemented?

The simple answer to the first question is, "You will not know with certainty and in advance that a specific enhancement will be successful." The idea that you can conduct a marketing research study to ask 100 or 1,000 customers their opinion of your potential product enhancement and receive a definitive answer regarding its success is little more than wishful thinking. No matter how favorable the initial reactions to the idea, there is no guarantee that it will translate into actual purchases in the marketplace. Likewise, customers may not fully appreciate the appeal of an idea or comprehend it when described to them in a research survey.

The only reliable way to know if a product enhancement will be successful in the marketplace is to actually test it in that marketplace. Until prospects are faced with an actual "buy" or "don't buy" decision or until customers can experience the product enhancement, they cannot really evaluate it. The good news is that in many situations you should be able to test the enhancement on a limited basis rather than having to introduce it to the entire marketplace.

We will move on to address the second key question, "How do we measure the success of the product enhancement once we have implemented it (whether on a limited test basis or across the board)?" We will not attempt to provide a comprehensive discussion of measurement techniques. However, we can describe some basic approaches to measurement.

Start with clarifying your company's objectives in adding the marketing communications-oriented product enhancement(s). Nearly all enhancements are aimed at

1. Helping to differentiate your product from competitor products in the category.
2. Increasing your product's perceived value.
3. Generating additional revenue.

Go beyond the obvious to ask yourself if your objective is to sell more product at the current price or to sell your product at a higher price. If the objective is to sell more product at the current price, will that be accomplished primarily by getting more people to buy or by increasing the volume and/or frequency of purchases among current customers? Do you hope to generate additional revenues from extra fees paid by customers for the enhancements or from other companies that pay to participate?

If the objective is to sell more product, then the second step is to determine benchmark sales levels for the product prior to the enhancement(s). What are the historic sales levels for the product in the markets/stores or among the group of customers where you will be introducing the enhancement(s)? How much sales history you need depends upon the product and the situation. At the very least, you should have a year's worth of sales history specific to the markets, stores, and/or customer groups.

Divide your markets, stores, or customer groups into "test" versus "control" categories. The goal is to define test and control groups that are similar in characteristics and sales performance. We suggest defining two or more each of the test and control markets, stores, or groups. That will reduce the chances of misleading test results due to the influence of factors such as weather, competitor actions, or economic conditions that might be unique to a single market or store.

Introduce the enhancement(s) among the test markets, stores, or groups. Monitor and evaluate results among both the test and control groups. If the test has been structured correctly, the control group results will show what changes occurred that were *not* the result of the enhancement(s).

The difference in the test group performance versus the control group performance will show the results of the enhancement(s). For example, assume that sales in the control markets increased 10 percent compared to the previous year while sales in the test market increased by 25 percent. This would indicate that the enhancement(s) was responsible for a 15 percent sales increase. The length of time needed for the test period will depend upon the product and the enhancement(s).

If the objective of the enhancement(s) is to sell the product at a higher price, one way to test this is to offer the product with and without the enhancement side-by-side in the same stores or on the same Web site. This presents the customer with a choice of "Do I want these hiking boots for $80 or would I rather pay $90 or $100 to receive the hiking boots along with an accompanying video or the added service of publishing my narrative and digital photos from my next hike into a commemorative book?" Customers then vote with their wallets and credit cards. This testing should be conducted in multiple stores or among several groups of customers so that alternative price premiums for the enhancement(s) may be tested.

The other way to test premium prices for enhancements is to establish and measure sales in various test versus control stores. The test stores should feature your product with the enhancement(s) and at the higher price, while the control stores have your regular product offering at its normal price. The same guidance discussed earlier for selecting and monitoring test versus control stores applies here as well.

The primary objective of marketing communications-oriented product enhancements should be either to increase sales of the product or to increase the selling price of the product as a result of increasing its value to customers. Success in accomplishing these objectives needs to be measured by comparing sales and/or profits when the enhancement(s) is added against what sales and/or profits are or would be without the enhancement(s). This applies regardless of whether you are testing at an early stage or measuring long-term success.

Measuring Additional Benefits of Marketing Communications-Oriented Product Enhancements

Increased sales and/or profits should be the primary means of measuring and evaluating the impact of marketing communications-oriented product enhancements. However, there are some additional benefits and methods of accounting for them associated with product enhancements. We will discuss four of these additional benefits and suggest ways of measuring them. Think of these as indirect benefits that can result in greater sales.

1. More Effective Advertising

Marketers that add significant product enhancements may find that highlighting those enhancements in their advertising increases the effectiveness of the advertisements. As discussed in the first section of this book, advertising that communicates real brand or product news is more credible and impactful. Advertisements that announce a new enhancement, emphasize the benefits the enhancement provides, and help to differentiate your product from those of competitors are likely to receive greater attention and generate better results than advertisements that are primarily image-oriented or just reinforce a company's brand message. If you regularly track responses to your advertisements, you will be able to measure the impact that ads featuring meaningful enhancements have on ad response. If you regularly measure audience recall of advertisements, you may observe changes on this measure as well.

2. More Publicity

Significant product enhancements are likely to generate more publicity for your products and company. Such enhancements represent news. The media want to provide news to their audience. The more remarkable or unique the enhancement, the more likely it is to receive strong press coverage. Major customer events like Camp Jeep can generate extensive press coverage. If your public relations agency has a good press coverage tracking system in place, it will be easy to measure the press coverage generated by marketing communications-oriented product enhancements.

3. Increased Time Spent With Your Company's Marketing Communication Tools/Materials

Some of the marketing communications-oriented product enhancement ideas discussed earlier in this section are directly tied to existing marketing communications tools and materials such as Web sites and product catalogs. Many company Web sites and product catalogs feature accessory items and other related products. Some of these products may be sold direct through the company's catalog or Web site.

When a marketing communications-oriented product enhancement causes customers to spend more time with the printed catalog or more time on the Web site, that translates to increased exposure to other products the company offers. And that increased exposure raises the opportunities for customers to purchase additional products. Additional time spent with the printed catalog is difficult to measure, but additional customer visits and time spent on the Web site can be tracked. Also, be sure to measure interest in and sales of accessory items and complementary products before and after marketing communications-oriented product enhancements are implemented.

4. Word-of-Mouth Communications

The addition of meaningful enhancements is one of the surest ways to increase positive word-of-mouth communications, customer referrals, and other *Communications From Trusted Sources*. The more remarkable the enhancements, the more comments (remarks) customers are likely to make. If your company has a structured customer-referral program in place, you may see a measurable increase in customer-referral activity upon adding meaningful product enhancements. Also, monitor online forums, blogs, and other public areas to see if there is an increase in conversation regarding your product and company. These meaningful enhancements are likely to help improve Net Promoter Scores (NPS) as well.

CHAPTER **20**

How to Develop Marketing Communications-Oriented Product Enhancements

Let's assume you are now convinced that your company should explore using marketing communications to enhance the value of your products. So, how do you decide what possibilities to explore? How do you find the time and resources to pursue these possibilities?

Focus Attention on Remarkable Enhancements

Adding a small enhancement may be easy and worthwhile to do for a variety of reasons. However, small communications enhancements rarely will be perceived by customers as adding significant value to your product or differentiating it from those of competitors. For example, the addition of an e-mail newsletter or several charts of useful data to your catalog may make sense, but by themselves are unlikely to convince prospects to buy your product over those of competitors or to pay more for it. Instead, concentrate on developing enhancements that will dramatically improve the user experience when added to the product.

Understand Your Customers

It is important to ask your customers what they want from your product and your company. Asking customers for their input helps strengthen your relationship with them by giving customers a voice in their dealings with your company. Also, customer input lets you know what your basic product offering must have beyond the Core Product so that you are at least delivering the Expected Product. That is the good news.

The bad news is that directly asking customers may yield disappointing results when you are seeking enhancement ideas to expand into the *Augmented Product* and *Potential Product* areas. This is because customers may not be able to conceive of an enhancement unless it already exists. An exception to this is a situation in which the customer is already aware of an enhancement that is provided as part of some other type of product. For example, an individual who likes the photo-sharing feature provided by Harley Davidson might suggest that your company provide a similar service.

How do you get beyond the limitation that customers may be unable to suggest critical new product enhancements that do not already exist? As a result of work done by Malcom Gladwell (*The Tipping Point* and *Blink!*) and others, marketing research approaches based on cultural anthropology are replacing focus groups and other techniques in helping marketers to understand customers.

So, a more effective approach to understanding your customers and uncovering potential enhancements is to spend time among them listening, talking, and observing. Listening to a customer's frustrations and desires; observing customers purchasing, setting up, using, and discussing your products; and conversing with them about related subjects are more likely to lead to breakthrough ideas resulting in value-added product enhancements.

Pay Attention to Lifestyle Trends and Technology Developments

Want to get a head start on identifying and developing product enhancements that your customers will appreciate? Monitor lifestyle trends and technology developments both inside and outside your industry. There are many Web sites, books, magazines, and other sources that provide insight into a variety of trends. Spend some time analyzing those trends and what they may mean for your company, your products, and your customers in terms of the challenges and opportunities they could present.

Let us discuss three examples of trends that are occurring as this book is being written in 2008. First, **cell phone use** is now widespread and the technological capabilities of wireless devices are expanding. More and more consumers want to access information from their wireless devices whenever and wherever they are. Whether it is accessing store locations, product reviews, how-to tips, or demonstration videos, consumers will expect to be able to have this access for a wide range of products. There are a lot of challenges in making this happen, but if you are one of the first in your industry to implement wireless enhancements and you do it well, it could add significant value to your products.

Another trend experiencing rapid growth in 2008 is what is referred to as "**Life Caching**." People want to record, document, organize, and creatively present great moments in their lives.[1] Some companies that observed this trend and its rapid spread as a result of technology developments have been able to get a jump on their competitors by providing life-caching services to customers. There are still many opportunities for marketers to capitalize on this trend. Remember that life caching can take many different forms including print, video, audio, online, and wireless.

A third trend that nearly everyone is well aware of is the **aging of the United States population**. Some Baby Boomers are now reaching the age of 60. As they age, their needs and lifestyles will change. For some, it will be more difficult to participate in their favorite activities due to physical limitations, family obligations, financial concerns, death or relocation of friends with whom they normally participate, or other reasons. For others, aging and retirement will mean an increase in total available time. That increased time could be spent on activities that use your company's products or that time could be spent on other pursuits that do not stimulate more use and purchase of your products. Can you enhance your products through marketing communications to help older customers overcome challenges or stimulate them to devote more of their leisure time and resources to activities that use your products?

Use Internal Resources, Your Marketing Communications Agency, and Other External Resources

Identifying, prioritizing, implementing, and maintaining marketing communications-oriented product enhancements is time consuming. So, even though companies recognize that this is important work to do, many companies do not have the internal resources to do it all or even most of the work themselves. Further, a company's own personnel often have a limited perspective based strictly on the things with which they are familiar. And often, internal personnel may be reluctant to recommend ideas that are remarkable enough to represent significant product enhancements or major change.

Outside resources may be able to provide you with some help in identifying opportunities to enhance your products through marketing communications. Industry media, such as magazines, television, and Web sites, are often tuned into the industry and the audiences. Dealers, distributors, and other channel members may provide some insights as well. Regardless of the situation, be sure you find the resources you need to successfully enhance your products.

Your marketing communications agency may be a valuable resource in helping to identify significant marketing communications-oriented product enhancements. This is especially true if the agency is knowledgeable about your audiences and products. Agencies that work with many clients in your industry should be able to take knowledge gained working with other clients and apply it to your situation. If you think of your agency as only developing ads and literature sheets, placing media, and writing press releases, change your thinking and insist that they provide you with ideas to enhance the value of your products and customer relationships. If all your agency can do or is willing to do are ads, literature sheets, media placement, and press releases, find an agency that will do much more for you.

Endnotes

Introduction

1. "Brand Building—1st Step to Reinventing Marketing." Association of National Advertisers Blog, http://ana.blogs.com/liodice/2006/02/brand_building_.html (February 7, 2006)

2. Marketing Receptivity Study. (Yankelovich, Inc., April 2005)

Chapter 1

1. Edelman Trust Barometer. (Edelman, 2007)

2. "Media Metrics: Something You Can Trust." *Media*. (Research Conducted by InsightExpress, August 2005)

3. "The State of Consumer Trust." (Yankelovich, Inc., 2004)

4. Yankelovich MONITOR. (Yankelovich, Inc., 2003)

5. Forrester/Intelliseek Research. (Forrester Research, Inc., 2004)

6. "Driving Word of Mouth Advocacy Among Business Executives: The Eperiential Marketing Connection." (Keller Fay Group, April 2007)

7. Forrester/Intelliseek Research. (Forrester Research, Inc., 2006)

Chapter 2

1. United States Department of Agriculture (1992)

Chapter 3

1. Reichheld, Fred. *The Ultimate Question*. (Boston: Harvard Business School Publishing Corporation, 2006)

Chapter 5

1. Reichheld, Fred. *The Ultimate Question*. (Boston: Harvard Business School Publishing Corporation, 2006)

2. GfK NOP World Word-of-Mouth Study, (GfK NOP, February 2005)

3. TalkTrak (Keller Fay Group, 2006)

4. Gladwell, Malcom. *The Tipping Point*. (New York: Little, Brown and Company, 2000)

5. "The Economics of Buzz," (London School of Economics, 2005)

6. Customer Dissatisfaction Study (The Verde Group, January 2006)

7. WOM Influence Study, (Millward Brown, 2005)

Chapter 11

1. SPAM Complainers Survey (Q Interactive, March 2008)

2. Mail Preference Survey (International Communications Research, 2007)

Chapter 13

1. Reichheld, Fred. *The Ultimate Question*. (Boston: Harvard Business School Publishing Corporation, 2006)

2. The terminology of "Most Valuable Customers" and "Most Growable Customers" was first widely used by Don Peppers and Martha Rogers in *The One To One Fieldbook* (1999)

Chapter 14

1. Topps Company Candy & Gum History, http://bazookajoe.com/

2. *iLove Magazine*. http://www.ilove.com.au (Modern Media Concepts)

Chapter 15

1. Levitt, Theodore. *The Marketing Imagination.* (New York: The Free Press, 1983)

Chapter 18

1. Sierra, Kathy. Creating Passionate Users Blog. http://headrush.typepad.com/creating_passionate_users/2006/05/which_users_lif.html (2006)

2. "Retail E-Channel Experience." (Cisco Internet Business Solutions Group, 2006)

3. Camp Jeep, Chrysler, LLC, http://www.jeep.com/jeep_life/events/camp_jeep/

Chapter 20

1. "Life Caching." http://trendwatching.com/trends/life_caching.htm (Trendwatching.com)

Printed in the United States
146798LV00001B/1/P